Also by George H. Harrison

The Backyard Bird Watcher

Roger Tory Peterson's Dozen Birding Hot Spots

America's Great Outdoors

AMERICA'S

FAVORITE
BACKYARD
BIRDS

Kit and George Harrison

A FIRESIDE BOOK
PUBLISHED BY SIMON & SCHUSTER INC.
NEW YORK   LONDON   TORONTO   SYDNEY   TOKYO

Fireside
Simon & Schuster Building
Rockefeller Center
1230 Avenue of the Americas
New York, New York 10020

Copyright © 1983 by Kit Harrison and George Harrison

Designed by Eve Kirch
Manufactured in the United States of America

1   3   5   7   9   10   8   6   4   2

Library of Congress Cataloging in Publication Data
Harrison, Kit.
America's favorite backyard birds.
Bibliography: p.
Includes index.
1. Birds—United States.   I. Harrison, George H.
II. Title.
QL682.H38   1983   598.8'0973   83-11341
ISBN 0-671-46411-6

ISBN 0-671-67341-6   Pbk.

All the photographs appearing in this book are by the authors except those appearing on the following pages:
Sam Grimes: 65, 74 (2), 134 (top), 227 (top) and 229.
Hal H. Harrison: 22, 25 (2), 27 (3), 28 (2), 29 (2), 30, 33, 34, 35, 45 (2), 46, 48-49, 50 (right), 56, 58 (top), 66 (2), 68, 77, 83, 87 (2), 108, 113 (2), 114, 116, 124, 134 (bottom), 135, 137 (2), 154 (middle), 164, 165, 166, 174, 177, 180 (2), 181, 184, 189, 200, 202 (2), 206-207, 209, 213 (bottom), 214, 222, 227 (bottom), 228, 234, 251, 252, 256, 257, 258 (bottom) and 260; color photos of Northern mockingbird and American goldfinch.
Ralph Long, Jr.: 47.   Ray Quigley: 217.
Karl Maslowski: 36, 63, 70, 71, 88, 93, 101, 102, 120 (bottom), 148, 190, 224 and 225.
Karl and Stephen Maslowski: 238.   Peter and Stephen Maslowski: 191.
Steve Maslowski: 60, 90 (2), 153 and 172.
Leonard Lee Rue III: 82, 89, 96, 106, 115 (top), 120 (top), 143, 179 (2), 182, 186 (top), 194, 198, 201, 204, 205, 210, 220 and 230.
Charles Schwartz: 109, 115 (bottom) and 119.
Irene Vandermolen (Leonard Lee Rue Enterprises): 110.
U.S. Forest Service: 196.   U.S. Postal Service: 16.

ACKNOWLEDGMENTS

Writing any book is a monumental task, requiring the combined efforts of a great many people. When it is published, however, the author or authors receive all the credit.

We don't want that to be the case with this book, because we are indebted to a number of people for helping us make this book a reality.

No one was closer to the day-to-day work on this book than George's parents Mada and Hal Harrison. Authors of bird books of their own, they gave unselfishly of their time and expertise. To them we are indebted for moral support, technical advice, research information and many photographs, and for their review of the text.

Others who reviewed the text were Nate Kraucunas, Assistant Curator of Birds and Mammals, Milwaukee Public Museum; and Richard M. DeGraaf, Research Wildlife Biologist, U.S. Forest Service, University of Massachusetts, Amherst. We are grateful to Nate, Dick, Mada and Hal for helping make this text as accurate as possible.

We thank the bird photographers whose superb illustrations have helped make this book attractive and more valuable to the reader: Hal Harrison, Karl and Steve Maslowski, Leonard Lee Rue III, Ray Quigley, Sam Grimes and Ralph Long, Jr.

7

Ned Smith's fine bird drawings add a different dimension to the appearance of this book and we thank him for permission to use them.

The editors of the magazines for whom we work on a regular basis were most understanding during the final days of production on this book. They know the meaning of "deadline" and allowed us the time to meet it. Our thanks to John and Bob Strohm of *National/ International Wildlife* magazines and Tom Paugh, Lois Wilde and Mike Schwanz of *Sports Afield* magazine.

We are grateful to our son Pete, a student of ornithology at the University of Wisconsin, for his work on the "Food, Cover and Nesting Preferences of Northeastern Backyard Birds," printed in the Appendix. The information originated in the book *Trees, Shrubs and Vines for Attracting Birds* by Richard M. DeGraaf and Gretchen M. Witman.

And finally, we are grateful to our editor at Simon & Schuster, Administrative Editor Dan Johnson, who saw the value in this book and who has been most helpful and encouraging throughout its production.

KIT AND GEORGE HARRISON

To Roger Tory Peterson,
for giving us the sport
of bird watching

CONTENTS

PHOTO SECTION FOLLOWS PAGE 96

Watching birds through the window has become a favorite pastime for millions of Americans.

INTRODUCTION

Birds, the only other two-legged creatures on earth, have fascinated man since the Stone Age. The ancient hunters who decorated the walls of their caves made the earliest known drawings of birds, preceding even those on the tombs of the Egyptian pharaohs, where no less than ninety species of birds are represented among the mummies, drawings and hieroglyphic records. Bird watching or bird listing has a history that goes back at least 5,000 years.

Today, Americans who watch birds number in the millions. There are various levels of bird watchers, from the armchair birders who read but really do not watch, and the watchers at the kitchen window, all the way to those hard-core birders who will travel to the ends of the earth to see new species. Among the elite are the behavioral scientists (ethologists) like Niko Tinbergen and Konrad Lorenz, who became Nobel laureates.

By far, the largest category would be those who watch the birds which live around their homes. A U.S. Fish and Wildlife Service national survey published in 1982 indicates that more than half a billion dollars are spent each year in the United States to feed birds. My own *Field Guide to the Birds,* first published 50 years ago, has been credited with some of this explosion of interest in our feathered associates, which in turn have benefited from our largesse.

During the last half century, cardinals have extended their range from Pennsylvania and New Jersey to southern Ontario and Maine. So have tufted titmice. Because there are increasing numbers of people feeding birds, the winter survival of mourning doves, evening grosbeaks and a number of others has been enhanced. And the mockingbird is no longer a southern species. The planting of multiflora rose, considered by some a pest, has extended the relatively nonmigratory range of the mocker to the Great Lakes and New England.

But identification is only the first step toward knowledge in depth. Margaret Morse Nice, who watched the song sparrows in her garden in Columbus, Ohio, became one of the foremost bird behaviorists of her day. George and Kit Harrison, in this new book, a sequel to George's well-received earlier book, *The Backyard Bird Watcher,* select ten species of garden birds which they have observed around their home, and discuss them in depth. These birds are backyard familiars across the country.

There is a tendency of many good people to humanize the birds that come to their feeders or the shrubs in their garden; to regard them as pets—little members of the family in feathers. This thwarts a true understanding of birds. Birds have a psychology of their own —a personality, if you will—that differs from species to species. A chickadee is a chickadee, a robin is dedicated to being a robin. They are not inferior creatures, not underlings. They are what they are— and very good at it.

Read the pages that follow and look at even the most familiar birds with a fresh eye. Each one is a vivid expression of life.

ROGER TORY PETERSON

FOREWORD

Backyard bird watching has become a great American pastime. It may be the most popular—if unheralded—form of family recreation in this country today.

There are 83 million wildlife observers and nature photographers in the United States, according to the most recent *U.S. Fish & Wildlife Service Survey of Fishing, Hunting and Wildlife-Associated Recreation*. That's more than a third of the population!

Most of those 83 million are bird watchers, and most bird watchers watch more birds in their own backyards than anywhere else.

It should be no surprise that bird watching is the most popular form of wildlife observation. That's because birds are the most visible form of wildlife on this continent. Birds are spectacular, colorful, intriguing and easy to lure into our immediate surroundings. That is not generally true of any other forms of wildlife.

Bird watching has also become big business. When Roger Tory Peterson produced his all-new *Field Guide to the Birds* in 1979, it was the fourth edition of a book that has been around since 1934. Yet, the new hardcover edition was on the *New York Times* Best Seller List for 12 consecutive weeks, and concurrently, the paperback edition was on the Paperback Best Seller List for 27 weeks. To have the same book on both best-seller lists at the same time is most unusual in the publishing business.

Bird popularity was confirmed when these stamps broke the record for sales of U.S. commemoratives.

On a local level, bird seed sales have been incredible. The Schlitz Audubon Center in Milwaukee, Wisconsin, sold 74 tons of bird seed in a single weekend. The Wehr Nature Center, also in Milwaukee, sold 40 additional tons of bird seed one week earlier. In Cincinnati, some 400 tons of bird seed are purchased each year.

Last year, a single hardware store in the city of Ann Arbor, Michigan (population 107,316), sold over 2,000 bird feeders.

Why all the interest in bird watching? Because it is a pastime that is vastly entertaining, highly educational and relatively inexpensive. Indeed, there is no easier, more enjoyable way for people to relate to and become involved in the world of nature than to attract birds to their backyards.

But in spite of all the enthusiasm over backyard birding, relatively little information in popularized form is available on the personal lives of common backyard bird species. Most of us can identify a robin, a cardinal and a blue jay, but how many really know anything about the daily lives of these birds . . . their sex life, nest life, food requirements, movements, enemies, longevity and other interesting aspects of their natural history?

This book was written for people who love the birds in their backyards and want to know more about them. Each chapter delves into the secret life of each species. The information is a culmination of gleanings from scientific literature, observations and personal anecdotes. Much of the writing was done as we sat next to the office windows in our home, looking out at the very birds about which we were writing at the time.

We hope that these profiles of America's favorite backyard birds will give you an even greater appreciation and respect for those species that have given you so much pleasure. We believe that to know your birds is to love them even more.

KIT AND GEORGE HARRISON
Hubertus, Wisconsin

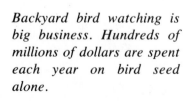

Backyard bird watching is big business. Hundreds of millions of dollars are spent each year on bird seed alone.

Backyard robin habitat includes open lawns, gardens, mature shrubbery and large trees.

CHAPTER ONE

American Robin—
The Classic Songbird

Only three inches away, on the other side of the kitchen window, the female robin sat motionless on her nest containing four blue eggs. I was making one of my frequent visits to a neighbor's house, where the robin had built her nest on a window ledge. I can still remember vividly how impressed I was with the concentration of that bird as she sat stoically on her nest while I watched wide-eyed through the glass.

Those daily visits to the Sefton home in Tarentum, Pennsylvania, many years ago allowed me to monitor the whole nesting cycle of one robin family. Though I was only a little boy at the time, that intimate experience with a family of robins was one of the early building blocks of my career as a nature journalist. It was a classic case of "the wonders of nature" seen through the eyes of a child.

There could have been no better backyard species to arouse my developing interest in birds, for the American robin, *Turdus migratorius,* is the basic bird against which most other songbirds are measured. "Is it larger than a robin? smaller than a robin?" etc. Though almost everyone knows a robin, its description is important because so many other birds are compared to it.

THE DEFINITIVE SONGBIRD

Specifically, the male robin is a 10-inch bird with a dark gray to almost black head, back and tail, plus its famous "red" breast. The red breast has been more accurately described in most bird guides as a rich, dark, brick-red color. The female is lighter or paler all over.

Though the robin is so easily recognized, few people have ever noticed that it has a white eye-ring and a white throat with broken black stripes. These lesser-known field marks were described, unwisely, as a means of positive identification in some of the early field guides before Roger Tory Peterson developed his system. The brick-red breast is a far better field mark. Another of the robin's lesser-known field marks is the white on the tips of the outer tail feathers, seen only when the bird is flying.

Though albino robins are rare, according to A. O. Gross, the American robin has the highest incidence of albinism among all songbirds. Melanistic or black robins are much rarer.

Many people are surprised to learn that both the American robin and the bluebird are members of the thrush family. But this fact is more believable when they hear the songs and see the young with their heavily spotted breasts, a characteristic of all true thrushes.

Our robin was given its name by early European settlers who, though not very observant, were reminded of the European robin, a smaller bird with a brick-red breast. Strangely, the European robin is not even closely related to the American robin. To make matters even more confusing, our robin is closely related to the European thrushes, including the European blackbird, a species which is in no way related to the blackbirds of North America. It was the European blackbird about which the nursery rhyme, "Sing a Song of Sixpence," was written, in which "Four-and-twenty blackbirds baked in a pie." Thus, our robin would make a much better pie than our blackbirds. Indeed, many an American robin wound up in a meat pie 100 years ago, when songbirds were not protected. One historical reference states that while on their wintering grounds, "enormous flocks were slaughtered in southern states."

Though most robins winter in the South, they are found at some time during each year in every corner of North America, from tree line at 12,000 feet in the Canadian Rockies to the hot desert coasts of Baja California. More typically, however, the robin is at home on lawns and in gardens across most of the United States. In fact, it has adapted so well to man's imposition on the land that there are more robins in North America today than during colonial times.

AN EARLY NESTER

Throughout its range, the robin is one of the earliest of all songbirds to nest. Records from Georgia and the Carolinas show that robins begin building nests as early as March. At the northern extreme, in Alaska and Canada, they are more likely to nest in mid-June. On the average, however, mid-April is when male robins tune up to produce one of nature's most beautiful songs and mark the beginning of another spring.

Only male robins sing. Though both sexes have calls and alarm notes, the male is the one who serenades us with his familiar robin song, *cheer-up, cheer, cheer, cheer-up,* although it does vary slightly from one male to another. Some ornithologists even claim that they can differentiate between singing males.

Anyone who has ever been outdoors before sunrise on a spring morning probably has heard a robin sing before any other species. It also has an evening song and is one of the last birds to stop singing before dark. And what a lovely song it is! Who wouldn't treasure vespers performed by a chorus of singing male robins? The thrush family connection then becomes very evident.

MORE THAN MUSIC

The song of the male robin plays at least two major roles: to establish and maintain a territory and to court a female.

It all begins in the spring when the males return to their breeding grounds, after moving north as the temperatures exceed 37 degrees (Fahrenheit). They are followed in a few days by the females. Robins, particularly the females, usually return year after year to the same area in which they were hatched. In the case of the male, if his home territory is filled by a more aggressive male, he is forced to seek another territory nearby. But as soon as the half-acre territory is established, the male will sing from every corner of it, usually from a height of about 12 feet where he can see well. The song tells other males to "keep out," for this territory has been claimed. The melodious warning is backed up by fierce attacks when another robin (male or female) enters the territory. Robins are very aggressive defenders of their territories. Fights between intruding and de-

This male robin spent an entire spring fighting his reflection in a Pennsylvania garage door window.

fending robins are common and usually end when the owner of the territory drives the intruder beyond the invisible boundaries.

It is during this period when territories are being defended that robins are sometimes seen engaged in fighting their own reflections in cellar windows and glass doors. The robin sees "another robin" in the glass and fights it in an attempt to drive it away. I remember so well the robin that fought its reflection in the window part of the garage door at my boyhood home in Pennsylvania. So persistent was that male robin that my dad nailed a little ledge to the base of the glass so the bird would have a place to perch as it "shadow-boxed" its reflection. Those mock battles continued throughout the breeding season that year, and the poor bewildered bird never did figure out that there was no real intruder there. Anyone who has this same problem and wants to relieve the robin of his imagined burden should merely soap the window or in some way eliminate the reflection.

When not fighting reflections or real competitors, singing males are courting females, for the song also plays a major role in the relationship between the pair. For one thing, it serves to keep the female informed about the male's whereabouts. When she is ready to be bred, she alights near him, chirps at him to draw his attention and then becomes submissive. The male will then approach the female and give his own excited call, which is usually followed by copulation.

A NEST OF MUD AND GRASS

Nest building is the next major phase of the robin's family life. Depending on geographic location, robins may take up to three weeks to build their nests before laying the first egg. In other areas where the growing season is shorter, they may be in a hurry and finish the nest in a few days. Five to six days is average.

Traditionally, the female robin selects a nesting site in a tree fork, on a horizontal branch or on almost any substantial ledge of a house or outbuilding, 5 to 20 feet above the ground; rarely on the ground. The deep cup is molded by the contours of the female's body and is made of grasses, weed stalks, strips of cloth and string worked into wet or soft mud and lined with fine grasses. The female carries the mud in her bill.

Sometimes female robins will become confused while building their nests. This loss of orientation will result in the bird's building more than one nest. I recall one mixed-up female who began building a nest on top of the coach lamp next to the back door of our Wisconsin home a few years ago. Our neighbor had a similar coach lamp next to his back door. Strangely, the robin built nests above both coach lamps simultaneously. She eventually laid her eggs and raised her family in the nest above our lamp. That robin was well organized compared to the one my father found one spring in Pennsylvania. That female built 13 nests side by side!

One pair of robins in Ithaca, New York, raised four young on the top of a crane which constantly swung back and forth to load cinders into a railroad car.

COMMUNAL NESTING

Other strange stories can be told about the home life of the robin. It is not unknown for two females to mate with the same male and cooperate in building a communal nest. One such nest was studied by a researcher at the Cornell University Laboratory of Ornithology. He watched two female robins actually build a nest together. They not only went about their work with little friction, but cooperated to the extent that one female stayed at the nest while the other female gathered the nesting material to be used in the nest. When egg-laying time came, both females contributed. A total of six eggs were found in the nest (normal clutch is four) and two others were found on the ground beneath the nest. During incubation, both females were observed sitting on the nest, usually side by side. Both birds spent the night on the nest. Though the eggs hatched, unfortunately the nest was destroyed before the young were old enough to leave. However, the same two females rebuilt the nest and laid seven more eggs. The report does not say what happened to the second nesting attempt.

Near Cincinnati, Ohio, another robin shared a nest with a cardinal (see chapter 4 for more details).

A typical nest is built of weed stalks, grass and mud. The average clutch is four blue eggs.

A loss of orientation may cause a female robin to build many nests side by side.

As tolerant as robins may appear, they will not allow cowbird eggs to remain in their nests. Cowbirds are the "lazy birds" that lay their eggs in the nests of other birds. Robins will usually remove cowbird eggs soon after they are laid. My father experimented by placing fresh cowbird eggs, one at a time, into several robins' nests that already had clutches of robin eggs. Although he didn't actually see the robins remove the eggs, they all disappeared or never were allowed to hatch.

THE CLASSIC BLUE EGG

Robins will normally lay one egg on each of four consecutive days, and then start the incubation period, which lasts 12–14 days. The oval eggs are unmarked "robin's egg blue," smooth and glossy. The female will do all the incubating, leaving the nest to feed only for periods of 5–10 minutes during the day. Meanwhile, the male sings, and is never far from the nest. This is presumably to be close enough to hear the female's distress call if danger is present. Again, robins are exceedingly aggressive in defending their nests against all predators, including man. Anyone who has ever passed too close to an active robin's nest knows that they are not shy and will attack fiercely. They will attack predatory birds, mammals and reptiles with the same vigor. It is interesting that when a nest is threatened, neighboring robins will voluntarily come to the aid of those in distress and help drive off the predator. Territorial boundaries seem to disappear during this brief "mobbing" of a common foe.

During quieter times, the male will occasionally feed the incubating female at the nest. He may also perch on or near the nest while the female is off gathering food for herself. Seemingly, both parents are constantly on guard for danger from predators.

HATCHING TIME

The first puncture in the first blue eggshell usually appears on a classic warm day in early May. It begins as just a bump on the outside of the fat end of the egg, but in another couple of hours, it becomes a rather large fracture in the shell cut from the inside by the chick's tiny egg tooth, located on the top of its bill. Slowly at first, the hatching chick pecks away at the shell at the rate of about 10–15 times a minute. Soon, the chicks in the other eggs begin cutting their way out from within their calcium prisons. During the whole hatching process, which takes about 24 hours, the chicks are still under the warm, dark, protective breast of the mother bird. In the very center of her breast is a special featherless "brood spot" which radiates the life-sustaining warmth so vital to both the eggs and the cold-blooded young.

Occasionally, robins will nest in a shelter or on a shelf provided by backyard bird watchers. This series shows the nesting cycle of one robin family from nest building to fledging of young. Here the male delivers grass which the female places into the nest cup.

Four blue eggs complete the clutch. Incubation begins.

Three of the four eggs hatch. Two days later, the female removes the apparently infertile fourth egg.

At the end of the first week, the three nestlings' eyes are open and feather growth has begun.

Nest sanitation is an important facet of daily activity. Here the female robin removes a fecal sac excreted by one of the youngsters.

Until the nestlings are capable of regulating their body temperature, the adults must brood them.

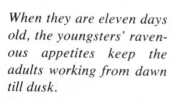

When they are eleven days old, the youngsters' ravenous appetites keep the adults working from dawn till dusk.

Immediately after this photograph was taken, the thirteen-day-old baby robins fledged. One flew over 100 yards on its initial flight.

When chick number one finally uncaps its eggshell, it is exhausted, blind and totally helpless. It is little more than an embryo.

The empty eggshell is quickly removed by the mother. She grabs it in her bill and flies to a nearby lawn, where she drops it or consumes it (probably for the calcium it contains), and then flies quickly back to her hatching brood.

QUICK FOOD SERVICE

It is about this time that the male robin arrives at the nest with the first meal for the chick. The food, though not very appetizing in human terms, is just what the newly hatched youngster needs: a half-digested cutworm. The tired chick instinctively holds its head up just long enough to receive the first offering from the male, as the female stands on the edge of the nest watching. She resumes her brooding when the male leaves in search of more food.

During the first few days, the male will provide most of the food as the female remains on the nest shielding the young from the elements and providing protection against predators. The food will consist primarily of cutworms, larvae of various kinds, spiders and earthworms. As the days pass and the young increase dramatically in size, they will be fed more roughage, including such interesting morsels as grasshoppers, crickets, maybeetles, leafhoppers, stink bugs and, of course, earthworms. The animal diet is supplemented with some vegetable matter including grass roots, clover leaves and the seeds of various plants such as roses, honeysuckle and plantain. The chick's weight will increase 1,000 percent in the first 10 days.

LET THERE BE LIGHT

On the fifth day of life out of the shell, the chick's tiny eye slits open for the first time. It peers out at the bright world for only a few seconds before closing off the strange sensation and retreating into the safer world of darkness. By the seventh day, however, it opens its eyes more often, having adapted to this strange new phenomenon of sight.

There are other interesting processes occurring in the nest. Though sanitation is a responsibility of the parent birds, nature has a marvelous system for keeping the young of many species from fouling their own nests. It involves a "fecal sac," which, unreal as it may sound, is a handy, carry-out, mucous sac that encases the fecal matter of baby birds. Robins are not unique in this. Almost all songbird nestlings employ nature's own diapering service.

Feathers actually begin to appear under the chicks' skin on the second day, but they do not grow out for several more days. On the sixth day, many of the feathers have broken through their sheaths, and the youngsters are beginning to look more like robins. By their 10th day, the baby robins are fully feathered and are capable of leaving the nest if forced. However, most remain in the nest for 14–16 days.

Exercise is an important function of nest life. During the first few days, the youngsters are quiet, but as the days pass they become more active and require more exercise. By the 10th day, the growing chicks have overcrowded the nest. They have also exhibited fear behavior by crouching in the nest when danger is near. By the 14th day, close to the time they will fledge, the youngsters stand precariously on the edge of the nest, extending their wings as though about to fly.

THE PLIGHT OF BABY BIRDS

Nothing is as cute as a baby bird just out of the nest, and a baby robin is among the cutest of all, with its spotted yellow-orange breast. This is probably the bird's most vulnerable age, for many fledglings are victimized by neighborhood pets and other four-legged predators, as well as birds of prey. Among the worst predators are humans who unwittingly create orphans out of baby robins. Millions of baby robins are picked up by people who either want to make pets of them or wrongly assume that they have been abandoned by their parents. It is a good rule to leave all baby birds alone, whether or not they appear to be orphaned.

During the post-fledgling period the male takes on a more active role in the care of the brood. He continues to carry food to them, protect them and be a role model for the young males. In the meantime, the female may be hard at work building a new nest in preparation for a second brood. Though it is not known how long the male continues to feed the youngsters, one observer noted that a 28-day-old youngster was seen 50 feet from the site where the female was building a nest. The youngster frequently begged for food from both parents, but both ignored it during the 30 minutes it was watched.

Continuing the saga of number one chick, if it survives the trials and tribulations of being a baby bird in a big world filled with danger, it will spend the balance of the summer living the good life. It will learn to feed itself, bathe in the neighborhood birdbaths, fight with its siblings and other young robins and grow into an adult. It will not stray far, as nearly 60 percent of all baby robins are still within ½ mile of their birthplaces two months after leaving the nest.

THE FIRST BATH

If you have never had the fun of watching baby robins take their first baths, you have a treat in store. They seem not quite sure how to get into the water, but they must try. First they turn their backs to the water and dip their tails into the strange liquid. That doesn't

Baby robins are among nature's cutest youngsters. Unfortunately, too many are made orphans when well-meaning humans adopt them, unaware that the parents are nearby.

do the job, so they try standing in the water. That isn't quite right either. So, they flutter above the bath trying to figure out just how to get wet. Finally, they just plunge in. Once they've gotten wet and have enjoyed the feeling, it seems that they are in the water much of the time. Just like human kids on a hot August afternoon, they never seem to get enough.

By late summer, all the young robins are eating the same kinds of foods as their parents: mostly earthworms (as much as 14 feet of earthworms a day, according to one observer), supplemented with such insects as beetles, cutworms, grasshoppers, cicadas, ants, termites, caterpillars, butterflies and a variety of fruits such as bayberries, cherries, grapes, pokeberries, mountain ash and others. A robin's diet consists of 40 percent animal matter and 60 percent vegetable matter.

EARLY BIRD SEES THE WORM

There used to a great deal of speculation about how a robin finds the earthworms it eats. Many people thought that it heard the earthworm because of the habit the bird has of cocking its head when searching for worms. The truth is that the robin actually sees the worm. It cocks its head because its eyes are located on the sides.

A LIFE FRAUGHT WITH DANGER

Like all songbirds, the robin has many enemies. Birds of prey are fond of plump robin breasts and don't hesitate to help themselves to one at every opportunity. Mammals such as squirrels, raccoons, skunks and opossums destroy a great many nests of eggs and young. The same is true of certain species of snakes, as well as neighborhood cats and dogs. Weather, however, is probably responsible for higher robin mortality than any other single factor. Cold, wet,

It is not unusual for robins to nest near people. This one selected a spot above a busy front door.

Baby robins spend the rest of the summer growing up and enjoying life, like this youngster at a birdbath. The spotted breast is retained until the fall molt.

stormy weather during the nesting season is a killer, causing a whopping 80 percent or higher loss of nestlings.

By September, our friend chick number one is a full-grown sub-adult robin. It has replaced its juvenal spotted breast and short tail with a dull brick-red breast and long tail. As the leaves on the sugar maple tree where it was hatched turn to bright gold, instinct tells it that it is time to move to warmer climates where food will be plentiful. With flocks of other robins, number one heads south in October. Its destination may be as far away as Mexico. On the other hand, it may not go far south at all, for some robins spend the winter months in northern and middle America. More likely, however, it will winter along the Gulf Coast, perhaps in Texas. I can remember seeing huge flocks of both robins and cardinals in the Aransas National Wildlife Refuge near Rockport, Texas, in January. Great waves of them would rise ahead of us as we walked along the refuge trails.

Early spring snowstorms often cause high mortality among robins. Backyard bird watchers can help by feeding apples and raisins.

It was flocks like those that, during Audubon's day, attracted gunners and archers. "Every gunner brings them home in bagsful and the markets are supplied with them at a very cheap rate," he reported in 1841. Apparently, robins taste like woodcock and are very good eating. Today, they and all other songbirds are protected by federal law. Unfortunately, the same cannot be said for the songbirds of southern Europe, which are still being slaughtered by gunners.

If number one survives the winter and migrates back to his birthplace, he will, for the first time, find himself in an adversary role with the same robins with whom he spent the winter. First, he will have to establish his own breeding territory. That may not be as easy as it sounds, particularly if the habitat where he was hatched is filled by a more aggressive male such as his father. Therefore, number one may have to venture out into unfamiliar habitats to find an unfilled territory. He will search for habitat that will fill his unique requirements for food, nesting materials and a nesting site. Then, of course, there is the problem of attracting a mate. When, or if, he finds a suitable tract of natural habitat, unoccupied by other robins, he will then begin to sing the song of his father and try to attract an unmated female who is passing through. If he is also successful at that, the pair will start the cycle of life all over again and help to perpetuate the species.

HOW TO ATTRACT ROBINS TO YOUR BACKYARD

The secret to attracting any songbird to any backyard is satisfy their three basic needs: food, cover and reproductive areas. Cover is probably the most essential requirement for robins. Their preferred cover or habitat includes small trees, including conifers, and shrubs interspersed with mature trees. They also like open areas, such as well-groomed grassy lawns, where they can hunt for earthworms. The combination of lawns where they find food, small trees and shrubs for cover and reproductive areas, plus a canopy of larger tree species will attract nesting pairs of robins. The existence of a house and/or outbuildings in the robin's habitat will further increase the likelihood that the birds will feed, nest and raise young there.

During the nest-building period, a pan of wet clay placed in the backyard will enhance the possibilities of seeing robins. They will also use such offerings of nesting materials as string, cotton and yarn.

Providing food for robins may present a problem for the backyard bird watcher because robins don't readily come to feeding stations. Their food requirements are such that they have to find it in a natural state within the backyard habitat. About the only time that food can be provided for robins is in early spring, when they have returned to their northern breeding grounds and have been caught in a late spring snowstorm. Then robins might eat raisins, apples and bread put out for them by concerned people. I can remember a bad spring snowstorm in the upper Midwest several years ago, when robins were gathered along the roadsides trying to glean any kind of food from the cleared shoulders. Many robins died that spring after being hit by cars, some because they were so drunk from eating fermented berries that they could not get out of the cars' way. Others starved. During that kind of weather, robins will respond to backyard feeding and great numbers of the birds can be saved.

Water is very important in attracting robins to the backyard. Any birdbath will do, but baths with moving water have a magnetic attraction for robins during hot summer days. We have two recirculating ponds in our yard, each with multiple levels to which the water cascades. The sound and sight of moving water is very effective in attracting robins of all ages which, to our great pleasure, drink and bathe by the hour. I remember the day we counted nine baby robins all bathing at the same time in the same pond.

There is one other possible way to attract robins to the backyard: by erecting a robin shelter. Though robins will not nest in conventional birdhouses, they may use a man-made shelf consisting of a roof, floor and back wall, placed under the eaves of a building or against the trunk of a shade tree. Though the robins in our Wisconsin backyard have totally ignored the shelters we have erected, the same kind were used frequently by robins in our western Pennsylvania backyard.

REGIONAL EQUIVALENTS OF THE ROBIN

There is one other robin in North America, the clay-colored *(Turdus grayi)*, but it is such a rarity north of the Mexican border that it really isn't worth treating here in detail. It resembles the American robin in appearance and habits, but is much paler. I have seen it at the Santa Ana National Wildlife Refuge along the Rio Grande River near McAllen, Texas, which is about the only place it can be seen in the United States.

One other bird, the varied thrush *(Ixoreus naevius),* looks and acts a great deal like the American robin, but is a distant cousin in the thrush family. Its brick-red breast and gray-black back might lead the casual birder to mistake it for an American robin, but a closer look will reveal an un-robinlike dark breast band and orange wing bars. Common along the Pacific Coast, the varied thrush breeds from northern California to Alaska. It can also be found in northern Idaho and northwestern Montana. Ideal habitat for the varied thrush is the shady, cool, damp coniferous forests from mountains to seashores in the humid coastal belt of the Pacific Northwest. Winter finds the varied thrush as far south as southern California.

G. H. H.

AMERICAN ROBIN FACTS

Description: A 10-inch bird with dark gray head, back and long tail. Brick-red breast. Female paler all over.

Habitat: Prefers residential areas where well-kept lawns with shade trees, small coniferous trees and shrubs provide an abundance of food, cover and nesting areas.

Nest and Eggs: In shrubs, tree forks, on horizontal tree limbs or almost any ledge on a house or outbuilding, 5–20 feet high. Lays 3–4 oval-shaped, smooth-shelled, glossy, unmarked eggs colored ''robin's egg blue.''

Food: Earthworms, cutworms, caterpillars, spiders, grasshoppers and other insects, plus a variety of fruit such as cherries, grapes, pokeberries and bayberries.

Life Span: Rarely more than 5 years in the wild; average 1½ years. In captivity, as long as 17 years.

Song: A clear caroling of short phrases which rise and fall, *cheer-up, cheer, cheer, cheer-up.*

State Bird: Connecticut, Michigan and Wisconsin.

Ideal nesting habitat for the black-capped chickadee is deciduous and coniferous woodlands such as these birches and spruces.

CHAPTER TWO

Black-capped Chickadee—
A Mini-Acrobat

If there is such a thing as reincarnation, I want to come back as a chickadee. Of all the birds in the world, none appeals to me more than this feathered ball of dynamite with the always-sunny disposition.

No matter what time of the year, be it subzero January or a hot, humid day in August, the perky chickadees are always flitting about, seemingly cheerful and unconcerned about anything but finding a fit sunflower seed at the feeder.

This winsome mite never misses a day at our feeding station. Whenever a chickadee comes to the feeder attached to my office window, I hear it land. It does so with a definite *thud*. I often wonder how a diminutive ⅓-ounce ball of fluff can land so noisily. Snatching a sunflower seed, it flits away on whirring wings, audible even through two thicknesses of window glass. Perching on a tree limb or on the grapevine, with the seed held firmly in its toes, the chickadee opens the seed by a series of quick thrusts with its sharp bill. As soon as the nutmeat is free, the chickadee gobbles it down, drops the shell to the ground, and again I hear *whir, thud, whir*. All this activity is punctuated by a number of *dee-dee-dees* as the bird carries on an almost constant chatter with flockmates.

A DAPPER DRESSER

Attired in its year-round costume of jaunty black cap, impeccable black bib and striking white cheek patches, this fluffy round bird measures only 5½ inches from bill tip to tailtip and weighs a mere 10 or 11 grams (about ⅓ ounce). To see just how light this is, Dr. Charles R. Smith of the Laboratory of Ornithology, Cornell University, suggests: "Take four pennies from your pocket or purse and heft them in the palm of your hand. Those four pennies are about the weight of the average black-capped chickadee."

Found throughout the northern half of the lower United States, Canada and Alaska, the black-capped chickadee is the most familiar of the chickadee clan, which includes 10 species throughout North America.

A CHICKADEE'S FANCY

Like most songbirds, chickadees respond to the change of seasons—and spring is the peak of its year. The little bands of chickadees that have been together during the winter start to disperse into pairs. It's at this time of the year that a favorite poem of Wisconsin bird bander Harold Wilson comes to mind:

> *Here's to the little chickadee;*
> *the sexes are alike, you see.*
> *It's hard to tell the she from he;*
> *but he can tell . . . and so can she!*

It's true that to us the sexes look identical. In most other birds in which the male and female wear the same plumage, we can usually tell which is the male because he is the one that sings. However, this doesn't help a bit in determining he from she among chickadees, because their elfin whistle, a plaintive *phee-bee,* is uttered by both sexes.

The pert black-capped chickadee is the darling of the feeding station.

A LOW-KEY LOVE LIFE

Chickadee courtship is not dramatic. The pairs, some mated for life, just quietly go off together to select a nesting site, with what appears to be total contentment and complete mutual understanding.

Of course, some special attention is paid to the female by the male at this time. He often brings her tasty morsels which he offers to her as a kind of gift. In the vicinity of their nest, the male defends a territory that may include as much as 8–17 acres.

Early one spring, a pair kept us amused for some time at our Wisconsin home. We watched them through one window, then another, following their movements as they investigated potential building sites. They went to every one of the dozen birdhouses on our property. Each that could be entered was inspected. (The wren house entrance holes were too small.) They even examined the hole in the hub of an old wagon wheel at our back door.

Where the pair finally settled is a mystery to us. They might have used a natural cavity, an abandoned woodpecker hole, or a birdhouse in someone else's yard. Usually, chickadees dig a hole in the soft, rotting wood of a dead tree stub, 4–10 feet above the ground. Working at the same time, but alternately, each bird digs out a billful of wood chips and flies away, scattering them around the woodland so attention is not drawn to their nest by a pile of wood chips. When excavation is completed, the entrance hole will be 1⅜ inches in diameter, and the cavity will be 5–8 inches deep.

It takes the pair a week to ten days to prepare the cavity. Then, during the next three or four days, the female creates the actual nest bed, lining the bottom of the depression with a blanket of warm, soft materials such as rabbit fur, feathers, insect cocoons, cottony plant fibers, wool and moss.

When the cozy nursery is furnished to her satisfaction, the female lays one egg a day for six to eight days. She may lay up to ten. Chickadee eggs are white, with mahogany-colored dots, and are so fragile that they are difficult to handle without breaking.

When the clutch is complete, the female begins the incubation, alone. Her mate, however, is always nearby to defend their territory. He sweetly sings *phee-bee* to her and feeds her during her stint on the nest. Occasionally the female may leave the nest to look for food herself, covering the eggs with the lining of the nest before she goes. But she always spends the entire night on the eggs, with the warm brood spot on her breast keeping the eggs at exactly the right temperature.

During the incubation period, both parents are cautious and secretive, and dispel unwelcome visitors with a hiss that could be mistaken for a snake's.

Naturalist John Burroughs neglected to pass this tidbit of information along to at least one group of guests. "One day, a lot of Vassar girls came to visit me and I led them out to the little sassafras to see the chickadee's nest," he wrote. "The sitting bird kept her place as head after head appeared above the opening of the chamber, and a pair of inquisitive eyes peered down upon her. Presently, I heard a faint explosion at the bottom of the cavity, when the peeping girl jerked back and exclaimed, 'Why, it spit at me!' "

Bird nest authority Hal Harrison told us of another incident that emphasizes the chickadee's attachment to its nest. He discovered a chickadee nest in a small, hollow tree stub with a side entrance hole.

When chickadees are ready to nest, they spend a great deal of time investigating tree cavities and nesting boxes.

When the right spot is found, a nest made of soft, warm fibers will protect the six to eight white eggs.

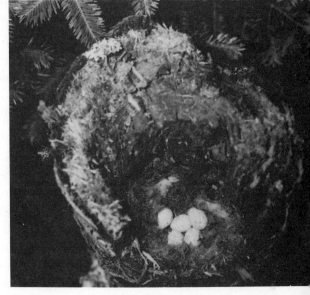

Chickadee babies require frequent feedings, resulting in haggard-looking parents.

One night, a fierce storm cracked the stub off right below the entrance, fully exposing the six eggs. Yet, the female, in full view, continued to incubate, and eventually the young fledged.

When the tiny youngsters hatch in 12 to 13 days, both parents feed the voracious chickadee chicks, promptly removing the fecal sacs to keep the nest clean. Fecal sacs are a wonder of the bird world. The nestlings' wastes are excreted in a handy, self-contained bag. It looks like a tiny balloon filled with white fluid. (Wouldn't it be great if human babies deposited fecal sacs instead of needing diapers?)

We can always tell when our chickadee "regulars" have a nestful of young. They come to our feeding station for a few quick sunflower seeds, perhaps a bit of suet, and then they are off again . . . and do they look beat! No wonder. During this period, they work hard to bring food to their ever-hungry young at the rate of 6–14 times an hour, depleting their own strength as they do.

When the offspring fledge at about two weeks of age, they look like clones of their parents, except that their feathers are brighter and they have an unkempt fluffiness because of some lingering down. Those roly-poly puffs of energy are just about the cutest things that ever came out of a nest.

For two to three weeks after they fledge, the chicks will still be fed by their parents while gradually learning to feed themselves.

If you have a summer feeding station, at this point you may be rewarded by a visit from the whole family. We have had as many as eight chickadees at a time at our suet feeder, all of them *dee-dee-dee-ing* excitedly while the kids watch mom and dad show them how to partake of the goodies.

Besides learning to enjoy suet (and later, sunflower seed and cracked corn) at feeding stations, the young chickadees follow their parents' example to achieve a balanced chickadee diet. They eat lots of caterpillars, spiders, beetles, ants, sawflies, gypsy moths, plant lice, wood borers, various weevils, tree hoppers and cicadas. To round things out, they also dine on wild berries. Their favorites are bayberries, some blueberries, and especially poison ivy berries. Overall, the chickadee's diet is about 70 percent animal matter in the form of insects and insect eggs, and about 30 percent vegetable matter . . . much of it taken incidentally with the insects they eat. Nearly all their daylight hours are spent feeding.

Chickadee parents are diligent about removing fecal sacs, the neatly packed droppings of the nestlings.

ACCOMPLISHED ACROBATS

While developing their flight skills, chickadee youngsters learn acrobatics as well. Right side up or upside down makes no difference. The nimble chickadee is comfortable at nearly any angle.

This ability enables chickadees to find food in places that other foragers overlook. They continually use their small, sharp bills to pry under bark and poke into tiny crevices where insects might hide.

"I once saw a chickadee attempting to hold a monster caterpillar, which proved too strong for it," commented ornithologist Edward Forbush. "The great worm writhed out of the confining grasp and fell to the ground, but the little bird followed, caught it, whipped it over a twig, and swinging underneath, caught each end of the caterpillar with a foot, and so held it fast over the twig by superior

A lineup of cotton balls, this chickadee brood has just fledged.

weight, and proceeded, while hanging back downward, to dissect its prey. This is one of the most skillful acrobatic feats that a bird can perform—although I have seen chickadees drop over backward from a branch, in pursuit of an insect, catch it, and, turning an almost complete somersault in the air, strike right side up again on the leaning trunk of the tree,'' he continued. ''Indeed, the complete somersault is an everyday accomplishment of this gifted little fowl, and it often swings completely round a branch, like a human acrobat taking the 'giant swing.' ''

Chickadees are also adept at flight maneuvers. It has been claimed they can change directions in midair in ³⁄₁₀₀ of a second—a distinct advantage in trying to elude airborne enemies like bird-hunting hawks, owls and shrikes. These predators take their share of chickadees, but the little sprites are such agile fliers that they usually escape a determined predator. Often, the chickadee will dive into

Their favorite food is sunflower seed, but they're also fond of doughnuts.

Surprisingly, chickadees are also quite fond of poison ivy berries.

the protection of a thicket or cedar where the raptor cannot follow, then will flit from one branch to another to further evade its pursuer. After a while the predator tires of the hide-and-seek game and looks elsewhere for dinner.

Nevertheless, the fast, small hawks are certainly counted among the chickadee's most dangerous enemies. But mammals such as weasels, squirrels and chipmunks have to be reckoned with, too, particularly during the nesting season. These small animals can sometimes get into the chickadee's nesting den or tear through the surrounding soft, rotting wood to get to the eggs or nestlings.

It's not surprising, then, that chickadees, like most songbirds, have a mortality rate of about 70 percent, although some estimates run as high as 80 percent. That means that seven or eight out of every ten chickadees hatched will not survive their first year. But nature seems to compensate for these losses by the large numbers of eggs that are laid and the fact that most chickadee pairs raise two broods each summer.

Among the survivors, some live for what seems to be a very long time indeed for such small creatures. Bird banders have reported chickadees that were certainly senior citizens. One was nearly 11 years old. Another, banded in Bedford, New Hampshire, was caught again and released in the same area when it was 12 years, 5 months old!

One of the most famous long-lived chickadees has to be Aldo Leopold's no. 65290, a bird he captured repeatedly in his bird banding traps. In fact, 65290 was recaught in Leopold's traps during five consecutive winters, a fact which deepened his conviction that the bird had a genius for survival.

Over the years, you may spot a chickadee or two that, like no. 65290, sports a leg band. A leg band is a fairly inconspicuous metal ring that has been carefully fastened to the bird's leg by a licensed bird bander. These people have undergone extensive apprenticeships and testing before being issued a banding permit. If you notice a band on a chickadee, you'll realize that it's nearly impossible to read the tiny numbers. If, on the other hand, you find a dead bird that is banded, send the band, or at least the number, along with information on the species and the date and the location where you found the bird, to the U.S. Fish and Wildlife Service, Patuxent, Maryland 20811. They will respond by sending you the information which has been accumulated on that individual bird. For example, they should be able to tell you when and where the bird was originally banded, and the bird's estimated age at the time. Your report will become part of the bird's record.

Though banders do their best work during spring and fall migration periods, chickadees generally don't migrate—certainly not in the sense that a robin migrates south from northern states or Canada. But chickadees do move around a lot when the weather starts to change in the fall. By the time the autumn leaves fall, chickadees have formed small flocks of two or three families. Usually these roving bands consist of from eight to twelve birds, and they stay together the entire winter, foraging in the woodland with all the carefree abandon of children frolicking in the winter landscape.

Chickadees are so adept at finding wonderful insectivorous treasures stashed behind and under things that other species, particularly nuthatches and small woodpeckers, have learned that it pays to stick close to them.

Scrutinizing every twig, branch, pinecone or catkin, the inquisitive chickadees are constantly on the move, covering about ⅓ mile per hour. Often, they scatter so much that they lose sight of their companions. For this reason, all members of the band constantly call to one another with a bright *chick-a-dee-dee* so that those who wander too far afield will still know in which direction the flock is headed.

After gleaning in the woods all day, the chickadees select a roosting site for the night. They often return to the same vicinity night after night. Some birds snuggle into a dense conifer to ward off wind and snow; some find cavities to shelter themselves—one bird to a cavity.

We've always marveled that on the most miserable, bitter cold, ice-encrusted days, the energetic chickadees are out and vivacious as ever.

Just the other day I watched a chickadee pecking at a seed with its back to a fierce wind. The wind was so strong that it turned the bird's feathers inside out like a collapsed umbrella.

DRESSED IN THERMAL UNDERWEAR

Nature has clothed the chickadee well for its frigid environment. The soft down next to its skin is its insulated underwear. Over that, its outer contour feathers, tight and waterproof, are its windbreaker greatcoat.

Occasionally, chickadees and other backyard visitors will collide with windows. Most will recover.

If you place the dazed bird under a sieve, it is protected from aerial predators during its recovery period.

Nevertheless, like all small creatures, it does have to work at keeping its body temperature up by taking in enough food to fuel its internal furnace.

According to Dr. Charles Smith at Cornell, chickadees have a special means of conserving body heat. "A few years ago, Susan Chaplin, a Cornell graduate student, conducted studies of the biology of black-capped chickadees to determine just how they were able to survive cold northern winters," he explained. "In midwinter, when the days are shortest and the weather often is quite cold, chickadees have their greatest need for energy to heat their tiny bodies. At the same time, because of the shorter days, the amount of time available to them for feeding is limited.

"At the end of each winter's day," Smith continued, "chickadees have accumulated reserves of fat upon which they draw during the night to provide for their energy needs. It is now suspected that their body temperatures drop nearly 20 degrees below their daytime body temperatures. Biologists refer to this temporary state of reduced metabolic activity as hypothermia. The hypothermic chickadee, at rest during the night, with slower breathing and heartbeat, uses less energy to maintain its lowered body temperature and even can wake up the next morning with a modest surplus of energy-rich fat reserves to allow it to get started on another day.''

The fortitude of these mini-sprites is apparent in a recollection by Virginia writer-naturalist Dr. J. J. Murray. "It was only eight above zero when we started out on a Christmas Bird Count on Middle Mountain in Highland County, Virginia,'' he recalls. "We walked in three to six inches of snow all day. On Sapling Ridge, the wind was whistling. As we expected, the birds were very few. But chickadees were everywhere, having the time of their lives. We only found 169 birds in all that high country, and 63 of these—over a third—were chickadees.''

Chickadees don't migrate, but spend their winters in small bands foraging through woodlands and backyard feeding stations.

How can you help but admire such tenacious, voluble revelers? And, almost fearless of man, these pixies are probably the easiest birds to attract to a feeding station.

Sunflower seeds are their favorite food at a feeder, and if you locate the sunflower seed feeder in a little cover such as shrubbery or a few small trees, chances are good that you'll have chickadees visiting you regularly, year-round. It may take a few days for them to find your feeder, but after they do, you can count on seeing them as regular visitors.

Chickadees are so adept at clinging to things that they can feed from the hanging "satellite" feeders as easily as they can feed from a window tray or a hanging tube feeder. Whatever model you choose, be sure that you place it close to your viewing window so you can get maximum enjoyment from it. Feeders that are designed to be attached directly to a windowpane or a window ledge, like the one in my office, are especially nice. Believe me, chickadees are not timid about using close-to-the-house feeders.

Besides sunflower seed, our chickadees relish suet, especially in the winter. They also enjoy finely cracked corn, particularly during cold weather because corn is a good source of carbohydrate.

NOT MUCH FEAR OF PEOPLE

One of the things that endears chickadees to most of us is the fact that they are quite tame, and it's not difficult to train them to take seeds right from your hand. Although we've never tried to tame ours to that extent, we're sure it would be a simple matter. Whenever one of us ventures outdoors to fill our bird feeders, the rest of the birds scatter instantly. The engaging chickadees, however, reluctantly leave the feeder but remain on a nearby twig until we have finished our task. Sometimes, one or two flit in and snatch a seed while we're still filling the feeder.

One birder was able to tame several chickadees one winter. He started by throwing a piece of nut to a chickadee that was a regular customer at his feeders. The bird picked it up and ate it. "Then I held a piece on my fingertips, and he came almost without hesitation and carried it off; this was repeated several times," recorded John

Surprisingly tame, chickadees can be trained to come to the hand or to any food source.

Woodcock. "Two days later, he would perch on my finger and take a nut from between my teeth, or would sit on a branch and let me touch him while he was eating a nut. He grew very tame that winter," Woodcock wrote, "and would often swing head-downward from the peak of my cap, or cling to my lips and peck at my teeth. If I held my hand out with nothing in it, he would always hop to my thumb, and peck the nail two or three times, then hold his head on one side and look into my eyes, as if to ask me what I meant.

"I tamed several more chickadees that winter; eight out of twelve, as nearly as we could count, were quite tame," he reported.

Maurice Brooks, the West Virginia naturalist, used another method that also proved successful in making birds like chickadees and titmice eat from his hand, according to Hal Harrison. In his yard, Brooks built a model of himself with one arm extended and the palm open. For several weeks, he placed food in the dummy's open hand until the birds came to expect the handout in that place. When Brooks removed the dummy and stood in its place, the birds continued to come to the real outstretched hand as readily as to the model.

DON'T FORGET THE BIRDHOUSE

When the snow starts to melt in early spring—February or March —don't forget to provide a place for these darlings of the feeding station to nest during the coming season. Bluebird houses are fine, but the openings of wren houses are too small. A 1⅛- to 1⅜-inch diameter opening is ideal. If you put up several on your property, you have a headstart on getting the chickadees to nest in your garden. Be sure to get the houses out early.

RELATIVES EVERYWHERE

The black-capped chickadee is the common chickadee of the Northeast and Midwest. Its family name is Paridae, a group which also includes titmice. They are found worldwide, living in Europe, Asia, Africa and North America.

The saucy blue tits, great tits and coal tits of Europe are close relatives to our chickadees. They are the common species at English "bird tables" (feeding stations). Intelligent and agile, these European tits have become adept at pecking open the foil lids of milk bottles delivered by the milkman and drinking the top milk before the householder brings in the bottles.

Here in North America, there are 10 native species of Paridae and one introduced species, the varied tit. In the South, the Carolina chickadee is the common representative of the clan. In the West, the Mexican chickadee is found in the Southwest, and the mountain chickadee, obviously, in high regions of the West. The mountain, Carolina and Mexican chickadees all closely resemble their black-capped cousin, and in the case of the Carolina, the only way to tell it from the black-capped is to be sensitive enough to the slight difference in their calls.

The boreal chickadee, a bird of the Far North, has a cap of seal-brown rather than black, and the gray-headed of the Northwest Yukon is, yes, gray-headed.

Other North American relatives include the chestnut-backed chickadee, black-crested titmouse, bridled titmouse, and plain titmouse. These live west of the Mississippi.

A close relative of the chickadee, and common throughout the East, the tufted titmouse also nests in tree cavities and birdhouses.

The bridled titmouse is a western species found in pine-oak woodlands of the Southwest.

In much of their range, tufted titmice are as common as chickadees, and every bit as delightful to have around. With their beady black eyes and expressive crests, they are a joy to watch as they go about their daily routines. Like the chickadees, titmice tend to be quite tame.

Hal Harrison told us, "One spring I visited an old bearded hermit who was known by the name of 'Neighbor' Carnahan and who lived in a rambling shack in the hills near Freeport, Pennsylvania. While we sat in the yard in front of his hovel, a tufted titmouse made innumerable trips to Neighbor's head where it alighted and tugged at strands of hair from the old man's head and beard. Each hair thus removed was carried by the bird to a cavity in a nearby apple tree where it was building a nest. Neighbor always appeared delighted with the bird's use of his gray hair."

K. P. H.

# BLACK-CAPPED CHICKADEE FACTS

Description: A small, round, fluffy bird, boldly patterned with a black cap and bib and white cheeks. Belly is buff; back is gray.

Habitat: Woodlands, mixed or deciduous. Also likes small groves and thickets.

Nest and Eggs: In natural cavities or nesting boxes. Usually 6–8 eggs, white with mahogany dots.

Food: Mostly insects, plus some vegetable matter such as berries from poison ivy, bayberry and blueberries.

Life Span: If it survives its first year, a chickadee may average a life of 2–3 years. However, some have been known to reach 7 to more than 12 years in the wild.

Song: The courtship song is a light, sweet *phee-bee*, probably whistled by both sexes. Their everyday conversation is made up of variations of the *chick-a-dee-dee-dee*, for which the bird was named.

State Bird: Maine and Massachusetts.

Well-named, the mockingbird mocks, or mimics, the songs and calls of nearly 100 other birds.

CHAPTER THREE

Northern Mockingbird—The Gray-feathered Ventriloquist

Enough was enough! It was 3 A.M. and I had listened to that damn bird for more than four hours and hadn't gotten a wink of sleep.

Reaching down to the floor, I picked up my shoe, headed for the back porch, and threw the shoe as hard as I could at the black silhouette at the top of the magnolia tree. I missed, of course, but at least I had the satisfaction of stopping, for a few minutes, the endless torrent of clatter that had been pouring from that inconsiderate beast.

A classic story about a mockingbird? Yes, and true. It happened many years ago when I was working in Richmond for the Virginia Commission of Game and Inland Fisheries. It was one of those typical warm and humid nights in the South when, without air conditioning, one finds sleeping difficult. Add the clatter of a lovesick male mockingbird who is motivated by a full moon and an apparent need for a mate, and one finds sleep impossible.

At first, the song of the mockingbird was lovely to listen to, interesting to analyze, and often humorous when itemized. But enough was enough. After all those hours of being entertained, I finally did

what thousands of southerners have done for generations before me
. . . I threw something at him!

Indeed, the mockingbird is as southern as pecan pie, grits and
black-eyed peas. It is as much a part of the natural environment of
the South as magnolias and jasmine. But the range of the mockingbird now goes far beyond Dixie, having extended into Canada, New
England and the Far West. In fact, the mockingbird's present-day
range map shows that the bird occurs almost everywhere in the
United States except in the extreme Northwest and Alaska. It can
even be found in Hawaii, having been introduced there from California.

I'll never forget the recent spring day in Wisconsin when I spotted
the characteristic white-flashing wings and tail feathers crossing our
road. Though I had never seen a "mocker" in the Midwest, I knew
it instantly. Since it was not seen again, we assumed that the bird
was en route to its breeding ground possibly even farther north.

NAMED FOR HIS GAME

Very few birds are as well named as the mockingbird, for it does
exactly what its name implies: it mocks or mimics the songs of other
birds it hears. It also imitates many other sounds, such as a rusty
gate, a bell, a siren and a factory whistle. More than 200 years ago,
colonial naturalist Mark Catesby reported that "the Indians, by way
of eminence or admiration, call it *Cencontlatolly,* or "four hundred
tongues." Scientists later named it *Mimus polyglottos,* "many-
tongued mimic."

Another early colonist, Thomas Glover, writing in *An Account of
Virginia* in 1676, said: "As to the Mocking-bird besides his own
natural notes, which are many and pleasant, he imitateth all the
birds in the woods, from whence he taketh his name; he singeth not
only in the day but also at all hours of the night, on the tops of the
chimneys; he is strangely antick in his flying, sometimes fluttering
in the air with his head right down and tail up . . . ; being kept tame
he ils [*sic*] very docibel [*sic*]."

Naturalist John Burroughs apparently thought more kindly of the

The northern mockingbird is as southern as magnolia, loblolly and jasmine.

mockingbird's song than I when he described it as "the lark and the nightingale in one."

Beverly's *History of Virginia*, published in 1705, speaks thus of the species: "They love society so well, that whenever they see mankind they will perch upon a twig near him, and sing the sweetest wild airs in the world. But what is most remarkable in these melodious animals, they will frequently fly at small distance before a traveler, warbling out their notes several miles on end, and by their music make a man forget the fatigue of his journey." That was nearly 300 years ago and the "mock-birds," as the early settlers called them, are even more friendly today and, without a doubt, just as musical.

At one time, mockingbirds were widely sold as cage birds and enjoyed for their songs and companionship much as canaries are today.

Probably the world's authority on the song of the mockingbird is Samuel A. Grimes, Sr., ornithologist and nationally known bird photographer. Grimes began recording the songs of mockingbirds near his home in Jacksonville, Florida, about 15 years ago. He became captivated by the number of other birds' songs imitated by male mockingbirds. Grimes began traveling to other locations within the mockingbird's range to record the songs of other males. Today, he has the recordings of more than 500 mockers on 90,000 feet of tape. He has traveled coast to coast, from Key West to southern Canada, amassing more than 45 hours of songs.

Asked his impressions of the mockingbird's song, Grimes responded, "The plain gray bird of dooryard and city park so far outperforms any other bird on earth in volume and variety of songs and calls that he stands in a class alone." Grimes adds, "He is the virtuoso singer of the bird world—far superior to the lyrebird, which some have called the finest singer."

Shrubby vegetation in southern backyards provides ideal habitat for the nightingale of the South.

HE CHANGES HIS TUNE

Grimes claims that he recorded a bird in Harlem, Georgia, which changed his tune 310 times in 15 minutes and interspersed 114 notes and phrases of 29 other species among 196 series of phrases of his own song. (Another scientist counted 32 species mimicked by a mockingbird in 10 minutes.) "The song of the mockingbird is two-thirds his own and one-third mimicry," he says. Grimes produced a 33 rpm record titled *The Vocally Versatile Mockingbird,* published by Droll Yankees, Inc. in 1979, in which he gives the listener examples of 86 mockingbird songs that imitate, almost perfectly, the songs of other well-known species. I have a copy of the record and I find it an extremely interesting piece of work.

Mockingbirds are also famous for imitating such man-made sounds as a dinner bell. Grimes tells about a mocker in Louisiana which imitated a dinner bell so well that the "farmhands left the field to come in for lunch." Another mockingbird in Miami imitated

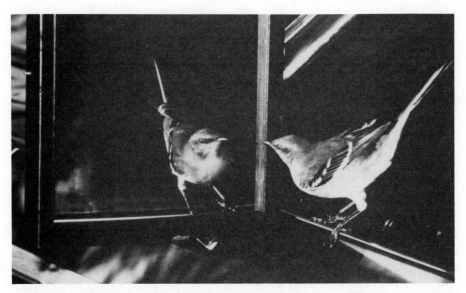

Defense of breeding territory often means that the mockingbird will challenge its reflection as though it were a rival.

Mockingbirds will build their bulky nests three to ten feet above the ground, well-hidden in dense shrubbery.

The three to five mockingbird eggs are shades of blue and green heavily marked with brown spots.

an alarm clock so effectively that a man living close by awakened regularly ahead of time. Another observer tells how a mockingbird in Nashville, Tennessee, did a first-rate takeoff of a squeak developed by a washing machine. Grimes' record album of mockingbird songs includes such amazing imitations as whistles, sirens, crickets and frogs.

Virginia's Dr. J. J. Murray claims that the mockingbird is "no mere plagiarist. He is a brilliant improviser who weaves these other noises into his own symphony."

JUST A PLAIN GRAY BIRD

It is difficult to believe that all that musical talent emanates from such a plain gray bird, but it does. Peterson describes the northern mockingbird as "Gray; slimmer, longer-tailed than Robin. Note the *large white patches* on the wings and tail, conspicuous in flight." From bill tip to tip of tail is 9–11 inches; wingspan, 13–15 inches. Sexes are alike.

It is the white flashes of the wings and long, white outer tail feathers which provide field marks for easy identification. Only the shrikes share this diagnostic pattern, but the shrikes' black masks easily distinguish them from mockingbirds.

Peterson also mentions the mockingbird's alarm call, which is a loud *tchack*; also *chair*.

LIVES CLOSE TO MAN

Mockingbirds are very partial to living around people, and are among the most common birds on southern farms, in cities and villages. They prefer nesting sites in such protected places as porch vines and house and garden shrubbery. Multiflora rose seems to be a favorite shrub, supplying both food and nesting sites. In the West, mockingbirds live in isolated shrub patches around ranch houses or in orchards or fig-bordered vineyards. In the Southwest, they live in sage and in such cacti as chollas and prickly pear.

Mockingbirds usually remain in the same general area throughout the year. They will establish two kinds of territories, winter feeding territories defended by individual birds and spring breeding territories defended by a pair. The breeding territory is usually established throughout most of the range in March or April, depending on geographic location. The size of the territory depends on the density of the mockingbird population, but generally one pair's territory would include several backyards.

A FEISTY DEFENDER

One of the mockingbird's well-known traits is its vigorous defense of its territory. The pair are always keenly alert to the trespassing of rivals or the appearance of predators. Indeed, the mockingbird appears to have developed a kind of spirit of play in its defense tactics. This is most evident when it defends its nest against intruding dogs, cats and people. It is well known for its "dive-bombing." Pity the poor dog whose kennel is located near the nest of a mockingbird. The pugnacious bird has been known to dive-bomb innocent dogs while they sleep or merely appear at the entrance to their kennels.

The ever-alert adult mockers are vigorous defenders of their nests. They commonly dive-bomb house pets that appear anywhere in their territory.

I remember the cat that lived next door to our suburban Richmond, Virginia, backyard. The resident mockingbirds made a hobby of threatening that poor animal every time it appeared in its own backyard. In fact, this got to be such a game that the birds would spot the cat coming out of the house and attack even before it reached the porch steps. After a few weeks of that treatment, the cat became paranoid and was afraid to leave the house.

Mockingbirds don't always have the last word with cats. William H. McHenry, writing in *American Forests* magazine, told of a cat named Blackie who sustained many attacks from a mockingbird while asleep on the back porch. However, the mocker made the mistake one day of attacking Blackie from the front as he walked across the street. (All previous attacks had been from the rear.) Well, Blackie made a three-foot leap into the air, and soon the only thing left of the bird were three gray-and-white feathers blowing across the pavement. This may sound like a sad story, but the mocker had its revenge. According to McHenry, the cat ate the bird, feathers and all, and the feathers and bones killed the cat!

POLICEMAN OF THE NEIGHBORHOOD

The mocker's vigorous defense of territory provides some benefits to other birds. It is a kind of "policeman," chasing away such predatory birds as starlings, blue jays and grackles. It will even attack squirrels, snakes, crows and owls that dare to enter its domain.

Certainly, man has no privileges with mockingbirds and is often attacked with the same vengeance. More than once I have heard the whir of mockingbird wings and felt the brush of mockingbird feet on my head as I approached a nest.

This same belligerent attitude is apparent in the mockingbird's defense of territory against its own species. In fact, the birds perform a kind of "dance" with intruding mockers which was once believed to be a courtship display. Instead, it is a confrontation of males at the border of their territories. The dance involves the spreading and raising and lowering of the wings, and the prancing of the birds as they face off like two boxers sparring in a ring. The

This rare albino mock-ingbird is still a stubby-tailed youngster beg-ging for food.

same kind of raising of the wings occurs when the birds are feeding. They look like mechanical birds whose wings are run by batteries.

It is during this period, when territories are so vigorously defended, that mockingbirds will fight their own reflections in windows, hubcaps of cars, or even a car's rearview mirror, as Sam Grimes found and photographed in Florida.

A BULKY NEST OF TWIGS

The reason for all this fighting is protection of a rather bulky nest, built in a small tree, shrub or vine, 3–10 feet above the ground. The nest is constructed of a loosely laid outer layer of thorny twigs; inner layer of dry leaves, plant stems, moss, and hair; and a lining of brown rootlets. The male first places nesting material in a suggested nesting site, but the female actually decides on the location and then both birds build the nest. They rarely reuse an old nest.

Records show that mockingbirds can build a nest in as little time as two days. But that is a minimum; a more likely building period is

A few months later, the fledgling has grown an adult tail and has learned to feed itself.

four or five days. When the nest is completed, one egg is laid on each of three to five consecutive days.

The eggs are typically oval, smooth, with a light gloss, in shades of blue and green, heavily marked with brown spots and blotches. They are interesting, beautiful eggs.

Apparently, the female does all the incubating, though there have been observations of the male guarding the nest while the female was gone for a few minutes to feed. In any event, the incubation period is 12–13 days.

Like other baby songbirds, the young are hatched blind and naked. They are helpless at first except for their ability to hold their heads up for short periods of time to accept the food that their parents deliver to them. Both parents feed the young, sometimes appearing at the nest at the same time. In his book, *Parent Birds and Their Young,* Alexander F. Skutch describes an occasion when a female mockingbird, the mother of four nestlings a few days old, was killed by a cat. Her mate fed the young faithfully, but he neglected the maternal role of brooding them through the night, with the result that they died of exposure.

First food for the youngsters is probably a cutworm or soft caterpillar. However, as the young grow, open their eyes and start to sprout feather quills, the food the parents bring them becomes more substantial. Such interesting morsels as grasshoppers, crickets, grubs and beetles are presented to the increasingly active youngsters.

After 11–13 days of care in the nest, the young mockingbirds are ready to fledge. They are very un-mockingbirdlike in appearance. Instead of the deep smoke-gray of their parents, the youngsters are more brown in color, particularly on the back. The most conspicuous differences, however, are on the breast, where the fledglings are not light like the adult, but spotted with a dusky color.

Young mockingbirds, like young robins and chickadees, are cute and almost irresistible. However, mockingbirds are protected by federal law, and it is illegal to keep them in captivity without a federal permit. Furthermore, most people are neither able nor willing to invest the time necessary to raise a baby songbird of any species, and most attempts end in the death of the bird.

People are not the only enemies of the mockingbird. It's a big world out there, full of predators, particularly for a fledgling. Despite its parents' aggressive behavior toward predators, a baby mockingbird is highly vulnerable to the ravages of neighborhood dogs and cats, as well as such wild prowlers as raccoons, skunks and opossums. Winged predators, such as hawks, owls and shrikes, also take a heavy toll of young mockingbirds, contributing to a mortality rate that runs into the 70–80 percent range.

However, the high mortality rate is offset by the fact that most mockingbird pairs produce two, sometimes three, broods each year, depending on the length of the growing season where the pair lives. If all the young were to survive an average of, say, 12 per pair per year, we would be up to our hips in mockingbirds, and indeed, in all species, in no time at all. So, it all works out in the end, and enough baby mockingbirds do survive to carry on the species.

Birdbaths of any kind are popular attractions for mockingbirds, particularly on hot days.

Mockingbirds can be attracted to backyards by plac-ing fruits such as apple halves where the birds can find them.

Berries are high on the mockingbird's list of favorite foods.

DIET CHANGES WITH THE SEASONS

As the babies mature, and spring turns into summer, the diet of the mockingbird changes. When fruit is available, it totals about 43 percent of everything they eat. Favorites include holly, smilax, elderberry, pokeberry, blackberry, mulberry, grapes, red cedar, black alder, bayberries and even the berries of poison ivy. In desert country, they love the fruits of the prickly pear cactus.

WINTER TERRITORIES ESTABLISHED

Diet is so important to mockingbirds during the winter that males and females will establish separate feeding territories. Pairs are less bonded as summer passes into winter, and both sexes will stake out individual territories. These areas are defended vigorously against other mockingbirds, though there is some tolerance of mates.

Little else is known about the changes that occur in the mockingbird as it prepares for winter. Perhaps some individuals which nested at the northern extremity of their range move south for the winter and establish their winter territories where food is plentiful throughout the cold months. It may be for this reason that some observers see an increase of mockingbirds during the winter months. A good example of this is the number of mockingbirds we have observed along highway U.S. 1 in the Florida Keys. It seems that every telephone pole has its own mockingbird. This dense population thins out when spring arrives and the breeding season begins.

INVITE MOCKINGBIRDS TO YOUR BACKYARD

During the warm months, breeding pairs can be invited to a backyard within the range of the species by planning and planting the kind of natural cover that mockingbirds require for nesting. This includes thick shrubs and trees such as holly, black currant, Japanese barberry, brambles, winterberry, inkberry, huckleberry, spruces, crab apples, red cedar and especially multiflora rose. These plant materials provide both cover and nesting sites for mockingbirds. Most also produce fruits that are readily eaten by the mockers.

During winter, if you have the right kinds of natural foods growing in your yard or can offer appropriate foods at your feeding station, you may attract mockingbirds to your surroundings.

Plants that attract mockingbirds include downy serviceberry, hackberry, flowering dogwood, common persimmon, mulberries, tupelo, American hophornbeam, pin cherry, black cherry, common chokecherry, Japanese barberry, northern bayberry and serviceberry.

Mockingbirds are frequent visitors to feeding stations that offer suet, bread and raisins. They are also partial to such table scraps as berries, apples and bananas. An empty grapefruit rind filled with just about any kind of leftover fruits increases the chance that a mockingbird will visit your backyard feeding station. In New England, mockingbirds have learned to eat sunflower seeds.

Water is also an important consideration. Though a simple birdbath will do the job, running or dripping water will increase the chances of attracting mockers as well as many other kinds of songbirds.

A backyard birding area in Thomasville, Georgia, used a garden hose buried and hidden behind a pile of rocks to spray a mist of water down over the rocks to a pool below. Mockingbirds, along with other birds, drink and bathe in the gravel-lined pool throughout winter and summer.

My father tells an interesting story about a mockingbird that followed him around his yard in Sanibel, Florida, while he watered the plants with a hose. "It would follow where I had watered," Dad told me, "and occasionally I would squirt the water on it. It flew just out of range and then returned immediately when I resumed watering the garden. Undoubtedly, the bird enjoyed this encounter," he explained.

A close relative of the mockingbird is the gray catbird, a smaller and considerably shier dark gray bird.

OTHER MEMBERS OF THE MOCKINGBIRD FAMILY

In North America, there is only one mockingbird, the northern mockingbird, but there are several other members of the mockingbird, or mimic thrush, family. Most common and best known as a backyard bird is the gray catbird, *Dumetella carolinensis*. This dark gray bird with a long tail, black cap and rusty undertail feathers is a resident of hedgerows and brushy areas around city parks and suburban backyards. It ranges throughout southern Canada and all of the lower United States, except the southwestern states and the West Coast. The catbird's most distinctive feature is its catlike *mew*. However, like the mockingbird, it has a repertoire of other calls and songs. These are more babbling and squeaky than the mocker's. The catbird is a little smaller and considerably shier than the mockingbird, but the two species are often found living in the same backyard.

Another close relative to the mockingbird is the brown thrasher,

Toxostoma rufum, a very mockingbirdlike bird of backyard and pasture shrubbery. It lacks the white "windows" in its wing and tail feathers and, instead of gray, is rusty brown on the back and striped with black on the breast. A bird of more open areas, the brown thrasher is also a mimic of other bird songs and sounds of man. However, the brown thrasher has a habit of repeating almost every phrase, a very helpful hint in differentiating its song from the mockingbird's. Found east of the Rockies throughout the United States and southern Canada, the brown thrasher is as aggressive and vigorous in its lifestyle as the mockingbird. A bright yellow eye enhances its strong appearance.

There are several other thrashers in the United States that are regional equivalents of the mockingbird. They include such western and desert species as the long-billed, curved-billed, California, Bendire's, LeConte's, crissal and sage thrashers. All are mimics to some degree and their songs somewhat resemble that of the mockingbird.

G. H. H.

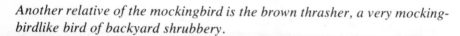

Another relative of the mockingbird is the brown thrasher, a very mockingbirdlike bird of backyard shrubbery.

MOCKINGBIRD FACTS

Description: A 9–11-inch bird with gray above and white below; white patches on wings and white outer tail feathers that flash during flight. Robin-size, with slimmer and longer tail.

Habitat: Thick shrubbery around homes, gardens, city parks and farms.

Nest and Eggs: In trees, shrubs or vines, 3–10 feet above ground. Bulky, loose outer layer of thorny twigs; inner layer of dry leaves, plant stems, moss and hair; lined with brown rootlets. Eggs smooth with shades of blue or green; heavily marked with brown blotches.

Food: Grasshoppers, beetles, weevils, ants, caterpillars, spiders, crayfish, sow bugs and snails. Fruits make up 43 percent of diet when available; berries, such as holly, mulberries, grapes, bayberry and poison ivy are favorites.

Life Span: Average after maturing is probably about 5 years. Terres' *Encyclopedia of North American Birds* states that a mockingbird banded in California lived 9 years; another 12; a hand-raised male lived 15 years, 4 months.

Song: Noisy, rollicking, endless series of sounds that mimic other birds' songs as well as some man-made noises.

State Bird: Arkansas, Florida, Mississippi, Tennessee and Texas.

The male cardinal is the only all-red bird with a crest, making identification foolproof.

CHAPTER FOUR

Northern Cardinal—
Big Red and His Lady

There it was again—the tapping and banging sound coming from the window in my office. It was 5:15 A.M. The male cardinal was shadowboxing again.

For three years in a row, Big Red went through this routine. Each morning he would fling himself at the window for an hour or two, letting up only to fight the cardinal he saw reflected in the window of our neighbor's house.

Aggressively territorial, cardinals start the nesting season by driving off any competing cardinals from their turf. It's not unusual for one to see its reflection in a window, think it's a rival, and fly at it over and over, attempting to drive off the intruder. Sometimes one will attack its reflection on a hubcap or in a car rearview mirror. One was even seen picking a fight with a piece of red cardboard.

Birds that do this don't harm themselves, and most eventually give up, although they may continue until the end of the nesting season. Ours was a little strange in that he began his ritual each October and continued it until the *beginning* of the nesting season!

In other ways, however, Big Red was a typical male cardinal.

Its heavy red "grosbeak" is used to crack the seeds and nuts that make up most of its diet.

Somewhat smaller than a robin (about eight inches long) and weighing just under two ounces, he was glorious in his brilliant red costume, accented by a proud crest that he raised and lowered at will, and a black mask at the base of his strong, heavy, red "grosbeak." That sharp beak has been the bane of many a bird bander. Cardinals not only use it to remove the aluminum rings that banders fasten to their legs, but often clamp it down painfully on fingers or hands as they are being banded, frequently drawing blood.

LOVED BY ALL

The cardinal's popularity is universal: seven states have chosen it as their state bird. It is known and loved by every child. The fact that the male is the only all-red bird with a crest makes identification foolproof.

Rarely do we see a male cardinal without its mate. Yet, many people don't recognize—or notice—this handsome fellow's lady. In her own way, she is as beautiful as he, but in a softer, more delicate way. Her folded wings, tail and bill are red, but her crest and the remainder of her plumage are more like buffy-rose, fading to buff on the underparts. Together, the male and female cardinal make a very attractive couple.

From the earliest times, people have been attracted to the cardinal, especially the flamboyant male. The first published picture of the bird was in a 1599 work by Aldrovandus, the director of a botanical garden in Bologna, Italy. The bird was drawn from life. Apparently it had been captured in the New World and brought to the director of a similar garden in Pisa, who presented the bird to Aldrovandus.

Later, male cardinals became highly prized as cage birds—even more than canaries—because of their loud, cheerful song and fiery plumage. Fortunately, they are now protected from that fate in this country, but not everywhere. We have seen cardinals, as well as some of our other colorful songbirds, for sale in Mexican markets. In small cages, feathers unkempt, the birds had a pathetic, listless look. They weren't singing.

That same sharp bill has painfully clamped down on the fingers or hands of many bird banders, frequently drawing blood.

As shameful as they are, those practices don't appear to be affecting the overall population of the species. To the contrary, cardinals seem to be doing very well, expanding their range farther and farther north.

Some believe that cardinals have been successful in their move northward partly because of the popularity of backyard bird feeding stations offering their favorite seeds, and partly because of a change in habitat from deep forests to more of the "edges" that cardinals prefer.

Cardinals shun deep forests, and are attracted instead to hedgerows, thickets, suburban gardens, parks and woodland edges throughout the eastern United States, west to the prairies, north to Maine and southern Ontario, and south to Mexico. They've also been successfully introduced in Hawaii. How surprised I was to hear a cardinal's song greet us upon our arrival in the islands!

Cardinals shun deep forests, attracted instead to hedgerows, thickets and suburban gardens containing dense shrubbery.

BONDS STRENGTHEN IN SPRING

Cardinal pairs usually remain together through the winter, often joining with a few others to form loose flocks. Toward the end of winter, the groups break up again as males claim breeding territories and either obtain new mates or renew their pair bond with the same female.

They begin well before spring officially arrives. Gradually, the male's behavior changes from paying little or no attention to his mate—even chasing her away if she deigned to settle in at a bird feeder that he wanted—to becoming quite attentive. People who have cardinals at their feeders have undoubtedly witnessed one of their courtship rites, a routine that can't help but elicit an "Aw, isn't that sweet?" from those who observe it. During courtship, incubation and even the raising of young, the male often solicitously feeds his mate. Selecting a sunflower seed, he cracks away the hard, unpalatable shell and tenderly places the sweet nutmeat in her red bill. She accepts the proffered seed and waits, in a ladylike fashion, for the next.

AN EXTENSIVE REPERTOIRE

Cardinals are vibrant songsters. No less than 28 different songs and calls have been counted for the cardinals. Only for a short period in late summer during their postnuptial molt, and again in early winter, does the male stop singing. It's not unusual in late winter, when the sun begins to gather strength, to go outdoors and be greeted with a chorus of *What cheer! What cheer! Birdie, birdie, birdie. Cue, cue, cue, cue!*

"Among birds it is not customary for a female to sing," remarked Dr. J. J. Murray, the Virginia ornithologist. "But the lady cardinal will often sing a whisper song, in form like the song of the male, but quieter, as if she were singing not to the world or even to him but for her own comfort and delectation. Her song is like her costume; it has a grace about it that warms the heart of every nature lover who is in reach of it." She also sings the *cheer* song, just like the male.

As the breeding season nears, male cardinals are more tolerant of females at the feeding station.

Sometimes the female will sing a phrase then stop while the male repeats it. Then he stops and waits for another song from her, which he repeats. If she changes songs, he follows, and they have even been heard singing duets in unison.

Besides the mutual serenading and the tender courtship feeding, cardinals perform a few other rituals during the breeding season.

One of the most common is a display in which the birds stretch out their necks as far as possible and raise their crests, which makes them look sleek and slender. Then, they sway their bodies from side to side as they sing, interspersing a bow from time to time.

When Audubon witnessed a male doing this, he wrote, ''During the love-season, the song is emitted with increased emphasis by this proud musician, who, as if aware of his powers, swells his throat,

This cardinal's nest, well-hidden in a thicket, is constructed of twigs and grasses and contains four speckled eggs.

Cardinals are sometimes unwitting hosts to cowbird eggs. This cardinal, however, buried the unwelcome egg, effectively preventing its hatching.

spreads his rosy tail, droops his wings, and leans alternately to the right and left, as if on the eve of expiring with delight at the delicious sounds of his own voice.''

For most cardinals, their territorial instincts are at a peak in early spring. Males competing for a territory or a mate might fly at each other several times, ''pecking and ruffling their feathers and uttering an angry buzzing note when in combat,'' one observer aptly noted. The bird that flies into windows and other reflective materials is doing the same thing . . . it believes it is battling another cardinal that has dared to intrude on its claim.

UP TO FOUR FAMILIES A YEAR

Cardinals begin nesting earlier than many other birds, and continue later, so they are often able to raise three broods a summer, sometimes four in the southern regions of their range.

By early spring, the pairs have formed strong bonds and territories are firmly established, so the first nest is begun.

Normally, the female selects dense shrubbery, a thicket, briars or perhaps a small tree in which to build her nest. Then, occasionally

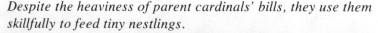

Despite the heaviness of parent cardinals' bills, they use them skillfully to feed tiny nestlings.

As with most other songbirds, nest sanitation is accomplished by removal of fecal sacs excreted by the nestlings.

assisted by the male, she gathers small pliable twigs, bark strips, grasses, rootlets, some weed stems and perhaps some leaves which she weaves into a fairly loose bowl-shaped structure. This is lined with fine grasses and hair. She may accomplish all this in as little as three days, but may fuss with it for as long as nine days. When it is finished, she is likely to ignore it for as long as six days before laying her first egg.

Cardinal eggs may be grayish-, bluish- or greenish-white with speckles or spots of brown in colors that have been given such descriptive names as "pecan," "cinnamon," "mummy" or "light mousy-gray." On some eggs, the markings are so thick that the ground color is nearly obscured. On others, the markings are sparse.

Three or four eggs make up most sets of cardinal eggs, but there can be as few as two or as many as five. Sometimes, the female will sit on the nest for a while after the first egg is laid, and again after the second, but incubation doesn't begin until she has laid a complete clutch.

During her 12 or 13 days on the nest, her mate continues to feed her, and in a few cases, a male has actually been seen sitting on the nest for a short period while the female was out for lunch.

In Kentucky, a cardinal and a robin shared a nest. Together they reared three baby cardinals and four robins.

These unusual photographs show the male robin passing food to the female cardinal, who in turn feeds it to the young.

REAL TOGETHERNESS

The rightful owners aren't the only incubators seen at cardinal nests. There have been several cases reported of cardinals sharing nests with other cardinals, even other species—surprising behavior in view of the cardinal's zealous territorialism.

In central Missouri, a cardinal pair built their nest in a rambler rose bush in which cardinals had nested in previous years. The female laid her first egg on April 2. On April 11, another pair of cardinals showed up and the two males fought ferociously. Yet, another cardinal egg appeared in the nest that very day. The next day, there were two more eggs (one was probably a cowbird egg). From then until April 20, there were two female cardinals sitting, or trying to sit, on the same nest. Each day they would sit side by side, but facing opposite directions. The eggs in that nest never hatched; this is believed to have been due to poor incubation because of the way the females were sitting.

But in at least two other instances, two female cardinals laid eggs and incubated them in the same nest, sitting in the same comical way—side by side, facing opposite directions—and in those cases, some of the eggs did hatch, and both females fed the youngsters.

One pair of cardinals and a pair of song sparrows nested simultaneously in a nest built by the cardinal and lined by the song sparrow, according to naturalist Alexander Skutch. "Both females laid eggs and both incubated and brooded, the cardinal sometimes sitting upon the smaller sparrow.

"Unless the nestlings of the two cooperating species hatch at about the same time, are of approximately equal size and require similar food, it is unlikely that both kinds will be successfully reared," said Skutch. "In the joint nesting of cardinals and song sparrows, only the young of the bigger cardinals were fledged."

In still another case, photographer-writer Steve Maslowski found a cardinal nest that was being used simultaneously by a pair of robins. "Three young cardinals and four newborn robins were all reared together. The four adults shared parental duties, though each species was apparently more inclined to take care of its own brood," he said.

BREAKING INTO THE WORLD

On the twelfth or thirteenth day after the female has seriously begun incubation, she may show a little excitement or restlessness. The eggs have started "pipping." Low, rhythmic tapping from inside the eggs means the chicks are struggling to make their entrance into the world. It is an exhausting process which will take the better part of a day.

The hatching chicks have special equipment to help them break out of their confinement. One is the egg tooth, which nearly every bird has at the time of hatching and loses shortly afterward. It is a small, white, horny patch on top of the hatchling's bill, capped with a sharp projection. In such a location, the chick can't use it to peck at the eggshell with the usual forward pecking motion. Besides, things are pretty tight inside that egg, and there really isn't enough room for the chick to pull its head back and thrust its tiny bill forward on the shell to deliver a good whack. Yet, it is necessary.

The other special equipment the chick has is a "hatching muscle" on the back of its head. This muscle seems to help the baby thrust its head backward, and probably helps the youngster, after it has hatched, to hold its head up for feedings.

Researchers have tried for years to figure out just what happens inside a pipping egg, but there is still a lot they don't know. One of their discoveries is that the chicks seem to go through a series of what are called "surge-pips." These are strong, convulsive movements that force the bill, especially the egg tooth, against the shell. Successive surge-pips weaken and finally fracture the shell. The tip of the baby bird's bill at last pokes through the small hole.

That's the hardest part. After the shell is pierced, the youngster probably continues its surge-pips, turning its body at the same time. In this way, the egg tooth cuts around the rest of the shell, finally allowing the tired chick to emerge.

While all this has been going on, the female cardinal undoubtedly has heard weak little peeps coming from within the eggs as her chicks penetrated their egg's inner membrane. This opened the air sac at the large end of the egg so they could begin breathing. She no doubt answered their little cheeps with some soft calls of her own.

Sometimes she stood up and peered down at the eggs to see just what was going on. Until now, the eggs had been smooth and quiet, even when she turned them a few times a day to allow waste gases to escape through the porous shells and fresh air to enter.

When the babies finally work their way out of their shells and into the nest lining, their mother stays on top of them, just as though she were still incubating the eggs. She is brooding them, because cardinal babies, like all songbird young, are *altricial*. This means they are not well developed. They cannot control their body temperatures and will have to be fed in the nest by their parents. Some birds, like ducks and pheasants, are *precocial*. Their young are ready to leave the nest as soon as they are hatched and dried off.

The tiny altricial cardinals, however, are blind, helpless and nearly naked at hatching, and weigh less than 1/10 of an ounce each. Their skin is reddish, but the soft, fuzzy down that is beginning to

Albinism in cardinals is rare, but not unknown. This female is a partial albino.

show on their backs and heads is dark mousy-gray.

For the first few hours after their ordeal of hatching, they are too weak to eat. It is far more important for their mother to provide them with the protection of her body while they rest and dry off. By brooding them, she protects them not only from chill, but also from too much heat.

As she broods them, she works at cleaning up the broken egg-shells in the nest. If bits of shell are stuck to the babies' bodies, she picks them off and eats them. She will carry away the larger pieces and drop them away from the nest when she goes on feeding forays. These trips begin when the chicks are several hours old. When they have the strength to lift their heads and open their mouths, the sight of their gaping orange-pink gullets will trigger a response in the mother. She will have an overwhelming urge to fill those mouths with food.

HARD-WORKING PARENTS

For the next couple of days, the male and female cardinal will supply food to their nestlings at the rate of three to four times an hour. Nearly 95 percent of it will be insects, mostly cicadas, grass-hoppers, caterpillars and beetles.

By the time they are three days old, the youngsters become al-most insatiable. The parents have to work hard to keep up with their demands, and may have to feed them as often as eight times an hour. Their instinct to feed them is so strong that they keep up the pace.

Sometimes, if a cardinal's nest is destroyed, or for some reason it hasn't successfully produced young, the overzealous parent will feed other young birds. In Illinois, a pair of cardinals lost their nest in a windstorm and started a new nest. Before the eggs hatched, the male started feeding a brood of robins that had just fledged. "We were amazed to observe the male cardinal and the male robin feed-ing one of the young robins," reported Stanley Logan, who wit-nessed the episode. "The adult birds worked in perfect harmony, foraging for insects or insect larvae in the immediate area and alter-nately feeding the young bird. During each of the next seven days,

Cardinals tend to wander quite a bit during the winter, but few ever stray farther than a few miles from where they were hatched.

the male cardinal was almost as active in feeding the four robins as were the parent birds. This apparently began a day or two before the second set of cardinals hatched and, once established, continued for a few days while the cardinal had young of his own. The young robins came to regard the cardinal as a third parent, recognizing with 'eagerness' his every appearance in the yard and following him for food.''

The most extraordinary instance of this behavior may be that of a male cardinal in North Carolina who kept seven goldfish in a back-yard pond well fed for a week. The fish crowded to the edge of the pool when the bird arrived with food, and got so excited they nearly jumped out of the water. Perhaps the bright color of the fishes' open

Cardinals usually are the first birds to arrive at the feeding station in early morning and the last to visit at dusk.

mouths was similar to that of his own begging young and triggered the response, or perhaps his own young had been lost and he had a particularly strong instinct to fulfill this phase of the nesting cycle.

BABIES GET FAT, PARENTS GET SLIM

By the time the baby cardinals reach the age of five days, they are able to digest somewhat larger insects and larvae instead of the tiny insect eggs, pupae, larvae and small, soft insects the parents had been bringing to the nest during the first days. As a result, the feedings may be reduced back to three or four an hour. Neverthe-

American robin

Black-capped chickadee

Northern mockingbird

Northern cardinal

Mourning dove

American goldfinch

Downy woodpecker

House wren

Blue jay

White-breasted nuthatch

less, the adults, in their frenzy to keep the little ones well nourished, are almost always hungry themselves. It's not unusual for the parents, tired and half-fed, to lose 10 percent of their weight during this period.

At about this time, the young birds' eyes are fully opened and they have developed the ability to maintain their body temperatures without needing to be brooded overnight. They snuggle down into the nest and keep warm against each other. For the first time since she began incubating the eggs, their mother can spend the night on a nearby branch instead of on the nest.

The youngsters continue to grow fast, and by the eighth day they are nearly adult size. They aren't ready to make their first flight from the nest, though, until they are about ten days old. At that time, they resemble their mother, but are a little darker. Their bills, instead of the rich coral of their parents, are blackish.

When the time comes for the youngsters to leave the nest, the parents perch a few feet away and call to the frustrated fledglings instead of bringing food to them. With urgent calls and food dangling tantalizingly from their bills, the parents get the young cardinals to make their first flight across the expanse.

Within a few days after that accomplishment, their mother will be preparing a new nest and laying another clutch of eggs, leaving her first family behind. The male will remain with them until he has taught them the necessary lessons of survival, including where to forage for the seeds that will make up their diet for the rest of their adult lives.

When the babies from the next brood hatch, he will again stay with his mate to help her feed the new family. The "teenagers" from the previous brood are on their own, but they'll probably stick around and beg for food from their parents if the opportunity presents itself.

By the time they are three to four weeks old, the young birds will start "singing," after a fashion, but it is quite different from the adult's songs. The song of the young cardinals is soft and warbling. Not until they are about two months old do they start to include a few "adult phrases" into their warbling.

After leaving their nest, the young birds start to eat a more typical cardinal diet. As adults, they eat about 70 percent vegetable matter, mostly seeds and waste grain, and only 30 percent animal matter such as insects. Among these are 51 species of beetles, cicadas, grasshoppers, crickets, aphids, ants and more.

NEST RAIDERS ARE WORST ENEMIES

Some of the cardinal's worst enemies are to be reckoned with in the nest. House wrens sometimes puncture their eggs, and snakes, cats and owls may eat eggs or baby birds. Even blue jays occasionally attack cardinal youngsters.

In some parts of its range, the cardinal is a fairly common victim of the cowbird. The cowbird is a parasitic bird that does not build its own nest. It locates the nest of another bird that is in the egg-laying stage and removes an egg. Then, the next day, it returns to lay its own egg in the victim's nest. In the case of the cardinal, the female cardinal generally incubates the egg as her own, and when the cowbird chick hatches with the young cardinals, it is fed and raised as a member of the family.

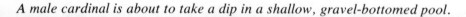

A male cardinal is about to take a dip in a shallow, gravel-bottomed pool.

AUTUMN BRINGS NEW FEATHERS

In late summer or early fall, usually in August, cardinals undergo a complete molt, losing their summer feathers to don their winter costume. The young birds emerge from this with plumage like that of their parents. The young females have the buffy-rose plumage of their mothers; the young males now have scarlet plumage like their fathers, although their bills remain darker.

PAIRS WINTER TOGETHER

The pair bond is strong in cardinals, and generally they stay together throughout the year. In autumn, they may join a small group of other cardinals, including young of the year and other unpaired birds, that will feed, travel and roost together during the remainder of the year. Sizes of these roving bands vary from a few individuals to many. We've seen spectacular numbers in winter flocks of cardinals in Aransas National Wildlife Refuge in southern Texas and also in Cincinnati, which has been called the "Cardinal Capital."

Cardinals tend to wander quite a bit during these months, depending on food sources, but they can hardly be called migratory. Most never wander farther than a few miles from where they were hatched. Yet, there is some movement northward in the fall and late summer, which explains some of the cardinal's gradual expansion into the North.

SELFISH ABOUT SUNFLOWER SEEDS

As they wander, they are likely to find the sunflower seeds and cracked corn offered at backyard feeding stations. Cardinals inevitably are among the first birds to arrive at our yard in the morning and the last to visit at dusk. Occasionally, they'll show up in the middle of the day, but usually only during severe weather.

Many people are blessed with small flocks of cardinals during the winter. "Some groups are made up of cardinals that are mild-mannered or only mildly domineering," remarked Margaret Laskey, who studied cardinals extensively. "Again, there may be one or more individuals that are pugnacious and continually driving their companions away," she continued, "either by running at them or actually fighting." The ones in our backyard seem to be of the latter disposition. We rarely see more than a single pair during the winter, yet friends who live nearby report having six or eight at a time at their sunflower seeds.

I've seen flocks of cardinals many times at Florida bird feeders, and have been struck by the fact that they all seem to be males. During the winter, a male cardinal won't share a feeding bonanza like sunflower seeds with a female, even his own mate. If she approaches, he darts at her and she flies away, not even attempting to retaliate. Shortly, though, as the winter days lengthen with the promise of spring, attitudes will change. The males will become tolerant of the females, and eventually even solicitous as the breeding season approaches. Then, when the female is nesting, the tables might be turned. If he makes a quick visit to a feeder during this time, she may not tolerate *him*!

Easy though it may be to attract cardinals to a backyard bird feeder, you may find them to be "spooky" when they're feeding. Unless they are very familiar with the feeding area, and with you, they are likely to be alert and poised to fly at the first sign of movement within the house. We think this seems to be truer of cardinals in the northern part of their range than those in the South. Maybe they just aren't completely relaxed yet in this new frontier they're forging.

But North or South, cardinals do have special needs when it comes to bird feeders. They won't use a hanging feeder that has small perches. They like to be able to have their feet on something solid. They'll gobble up cracked corn and sunflower seeds from feeding shelves or tables, or right from the ground, but don't expect them to use the type of feeder that is so successful with chickadees and finches. The exception to this is a Droll Yankee or similar tubular feeder that has a seed catcher attached to the bottom. The cardinals will sit on the seed catcher (a large round disk) and eat the seeds it holds.

Getting them to nest in your backyard is not quite as easy, but if

Sunflower seeds are the cardinals' favorite feeding station food, but they're also fond of cracked corn.

you have a grape arbor, a thicket of multiflora rose, or an edge of dense shrubbery, you'll at least be able to offer them the type of habitat they're looking for. If you are successful, they'll add year-round excitement to your garden. Whether they are singing from the limb of a maple tree or cracking seeds with their powerful bills at the feeding station, most of us feel the way Audubon did when he said of the cardinal: "In richness of plumage, elegance of motion, and strength of song, this species surpasses all its kindred in the United States."

RELATIVES GALORE

The cardinal belongs to the family Emberizidae (the largest family of North American birds) in the subfamily Cardinalinae.

The cardinal's closest relative lives in the Southwest. It is the pyrrhuloxia, *Cardinalis sinuatus,* a bird that is easily mistaken for a female cardinal. A lovely gray bird with red breast, red crest and

Big Red on mistletoe—a perfect holiday image.

yellow bill, the pyrrhuloxia is found in the deserts and plains of the Southwest, from Arizona to southeastern Texas and as far south as central Mexico.

Other relatives are the grosbeaks. In fact, the cardinal was once called the cardinal grosbeak, and if you look at the size and shape of the cardinal's bill and those of the grosbeaks, you'll clearly see why. The most common grosbeaks are the rose-breasted grosbeak, *Pheucticus ludovicianus,* and the evening grosbeak, *Coccothraustes vespertina.* The rose-breasted grosbeak is a summer bird in our country. It breeds from northeastern British Columbia to Nova Scotia, south to Kansas and Georgia. The female is streaked brown; the male has a rosy-red triangular breast patch, black upperparts, black wings with white patches, and white belly and rump. In fall, the male resembles the female, except that it still has black wings and

That the evening grosbeak is related to the cardinal is evident in the similarity of their heavy bills.

tail. The rose-breasted grosbeak winters in the West Indies and from Mexico south to Peru.

The evening grosbeak is best known as a winter visitor that descends in large flocks on backyard feeding stations, devouring sunflower seeds at an astonishing rate. If you have a visit from these lovely birds that look like overgrown goldfinches, you'll no doubt have to fill your feeders several times a day to keep up with them. The females are silvery with tinges of yellow, and have black-and-white wings and tail. The male is dull yellow with a black cap and tail and black-and-white wings. Evening grosbeaks breed as far north as northern British Columbia and New Brunswick and spend the winter as far south as southern California and even Mexico. Having them at their feeders in the winter is one of those things birders like to use in games of one-upmanship with other birders who maintain feeding stations. To have evening grosbeaks eat you out of your last sunflower seed is to be the envy of your peers.

The blue grosbeak, a deep violet-blue bird, is fairly common in the South.

A less common grosbeak is the black-headed, a western bird found from British Columbia, Alberta and Saskatchewan, through the West, as far south as Mexico. The black-headed male has a rusty breast, black-and-white wings, a pale bill and black head. The female is streaked brown.

K. P. H.

NORTHERN CARDINAL FACTS

Description: There's no mistaking the male cardinal. He's our only red bird with a crest. Even his bill and legs are red. His only accent is a patch of jet black surrounding the base of his bill. The female sports buffy-rose plumage enhanced by rosy wings and tail. If you get a very close look, you'll see that she has red eyebrows! The female has a coral-colored bill, looking as though she had taken the time to apply lipstick before facing the world. Young birds have blackish bills, but otherwise resemble the adult female.

Habitat: Forest edges, open woodlands, suburban gardens, parks, thickets and hedgerows.

Nest and Eggs: In a thicket, brier or small deciduous or coniferous tree, usually less than 10 feet from the ground. There may be 2 to 5 eggs, but 3 or 4 is common. They are bluish, grayish or greenish, with brown markings that may be sparse or thick.

Food: Mostly vegetable matter, especially seeds and waste grain; some buds and wild fruits. Eats 51 species of beetles, grasshoppers, cicadas, etc. Especially fond of sunflower seeds and cracked corn at bird feeders.

Life Span: If they survive to adulthood, cardinals may live to be 3 years old or more. Oldsters on record include a male and female that lived to be 10 years old, a male that made it to 13½, a female to 13 years and 8 months, and the all-time record breaker, a cardinal that lived as a house pet in Atlanta for 28½ years, from 1933 to 1961!

Song: Is known to have at least 28 different songs and calls. The most common is the song of *What cheer! Birdie, birdie, birdie.* Sometimes *cue, cue, cue* will end the *what-cheer* song; sometimes it is used alone. Their alarm note is a sharp *chip.*

State Bird: The cardinal holds the record for having the most states select it as their official state bird: seven. They are Illinois, Indiana, Kentucky, North Carolina, Ohio, Virginia and West Virginia.

A mourning dove, fluffed against the cold, is one of an estimated 500 million of its kind in North America.

CHAPTER FIVE

Mourning Dove—
Bird of the Morning

As I write, five mourning doves are feeding on cracked corn only 10 feet away on the other side of my office window. It is December in Wisconsin and the doves are walking in fresh snow. Two of them are on the tray feeder and three are on the ground gleaning cast-off kernels. How peaceful they look; delightful birds to have around.

The mourning dove had to be one of the first birds to attract the attention of our early European settlers. They must have noticed how closely it resembled some of the Old World pigeons. Further-more, the dove's calls probably reminded them of home and made them a little sad.

The name "mourning dove" certainly suggests a bird of sadness. Its mournful *cooing* reinforces the impression of a melancholy crea-ture.

But the mourning dove, *Zenaida macroura,* has little about which to be sad. Indeed, it is one of the most successful of all bird species. Unlike its late, great relative, the passenger pigeon, the mourning dove is thriving throughout its many habitats. There are more in North America today than ever before in history. Latest govern-ment estimates place the population at something over 500 million birds! The reason the passenger pigeon didn't continue to enjoy this kind of success is simply that it was unable to adapt to man's intrusion on the land. The mourning dove, on the other hand, adapted beautifully and has actually benefited from man's agrarian culture.

A SONGBIRD AND A GAME BIRD

In fact, there are so many mourning doves in the United States that they have become one of the most popular of all game species, a subject that has created some friction between hunters and non-hunters. If you are a mourning dove admirer, you are probably in one of two camps: those who consider it a songbird and those who consider it a game bird. Regardless of which camp you are in, there is a great deal about this bird to enjoy, for it is a highly adaptable, amazingly prolific, extremely attractive species of field and garden. Mourning doves have so many good attributes that their abundance is a blessing for all of us.

Mourning doves breed in all 48 contiguous states, southern Canada and Alaska, a fact that is not true of any other game bird. They also nest south into Mexico and all the way to Panama.

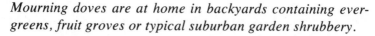

Mourning doves are at home in backyards containing evergreens, fruit groves or typical suburban garden shrubbery.

This male mourning dove is soaring high in a courtship flight. He will deliver the twig he is carrying to his mate at the nest.

MORE SUBTLE THAN SPECTACULAR

The classic wild dove of North America, the mourning is so unobtrusive in deportment that it is inconspicuous when compared to most other backyard species. This 12-inch-long bird with a small head and small bill is larger than a robin, but smaller and slimmer than a barnyard or city pigeon (rock dove). It is fawn-colored with pinkish-red feet and legs, black spots on its back and a long, pointed tail showing white outer tail feathers in flight. When it flies, it flaps its wings continuously, creating a musical whistle as the air passes through its wing feathers. A very rapid flier, the mourning dove has been clocked at 55 mph, with bursts up to 60. Leisure flight speed is 30–40 mph. It has the incredible ability to change direction and speed of flight with lightning precision. When it walks, the mourning dove places one foot in front of the other, jerking its head with each stride.

This threat display is common among nesting mourning doves as they defend their territories.

Sexes are alike except for a subtle difference in coloring. Males have a slightly bluish crown and nape as well as a wash of pinkish or rose hue on their breasts. The females are brown or grayish in those areas of their plumage.

A BIRD OF ALL REGIONS

Because the mourning dove is so common in so many regions of the country, it has no specific habitat. It is equally at home in deserts and rain forests, on mountaintops and treeless plains, in farmlands and suburban shrubbery. This undoubtedly has helped it survive man's imposition on the landscape. It is truly a bird for all seasons and all regions.

BILLING AND COOING

In most of the country, mourning doves begin their nesting cycle in March or April with their famous billing and cooing as "the voice of the turtle is heard in our land" (The Song of Solomon) and in backyards across America. The U.S. Fish and Wildlife Service estimates mourning dove populations nationwide each spring by counting their coo calls. Trained personnel travel established routes each year between May 20 and 31 and literally count the number of calls they hear. It is through year-to-year comparisons along those established routes that annual population estimates are made. A study conducted by the Missouri Department of Conservation showed that unmated males coo more frequently and have a greater probability of being heard than mated males.

Does a biologist get tired of listening to doves cooing? Like the song of the mockingbird, too much of the dove's beautiful melancholy call does become annoying to some people. We have never reached that point. We enjoy awakening on spring mornings to the sound of the doves cooing in the basswood trees outside our bedroom. For us, their call is as much a part of spring as the call of the spring peepers in the marsh.

That cooing is a very important part of the mourning dove's courtship. Only the males coo. The call consists of five to seven notes: one note, then a higher one, and finally three to five lower notes held at greater length: *coo-ah, cooo, cooo, coo.*

SOARING LOVE

Another important aspect of dove relations is the courtship flight of the male. Watching a performance of the flight on a spring or summer day is a singular delight. The male leaves his female sitting on a perch and flies high into the sky on strong, flapping wings. When he has obtained a height of 100 feet or more, he will set his wings and glide back to earth in dramatic, sweeping circles. The flight ends back at the perch, where his lady fair has seemingly paid little or no attention to his aerial acrobatics.

After pairing, male mourning doves defend modest territories that include the nest site, cooing perches and areas from which they will gather nesting material. All other activities, such as feeding and roosting, usually occur outside the nesting territory, sometimes as far as five miles away. This is unusual; most species spend all of their time on their territory during the breeding season.

A BIRD OF THE MORNING

The Missouri study also showed that the mourning dove would have been more accurately named the "morning dove," for most of its daily activity occurs in the early morning from about 7 to 9 A.M. It not only does much of its cooing and courting in the early morning, but also builds its nest and defends its territory most vigorously during that period. By noon, most dove activity has diminished to resting and preening, often done off the nesting territory and in the company of other doves. Later in the afternoon, activity picks up again.

Unlike the passenger pigeon, the mourning dove is not considered a colonial nester. Though mourning doves associate with other doves away from their territories and their nests may be within sight of other nesting doves, they never nest together in huge numbers as did the passenger pigeons. This is doubtless another factor which has contributed to their success.

Perhaps the custom of nesting by individual pairs has something to do with the fact that the availability of nesting material is an important consideration in selecting a territory. Another interesting fact that came out of the Missouri study is that without adequate nesting material the breeding cycle could not continue.

MALE CHOOSES NEST SITE; HELPS BUILD

It is difficult to understand why doves are so demanding about nesting material, for they build one of the flimsiest nests in all the bird world.

It is the male that selects the nesting site, often on a horizontal branch of an evergreen, 10–25 feet above the ground. He follows through by gathering sticks for the nest. He will deliver them to the female by alighting on her back as she sits on their partly constructed nest. This is thought to add weight and better mold the nest. But the finished structure never looks very finished, for it is a primitive platform of sticks so thin that eggs can be seen through the twigs from below. It has little, if any, lining of grass, weeds or rootlets.

One of the flimsiest nests in the bird world, the mourning dove's platform of sticks usually contains two white eggs.

Mourning doves will sometimes build their nests on the vacant nests of other birds. This one was built on top of an old grackle nest.

So nonchalant are mourning doves about the construction of their nests that it is not unusual for them to use the vacant nests of robins, catbirds, cardinals, blue jays, brown thrashers, mockingbirds or grackles as foundations for their twig platforms. If the doves' nest is successful, they will often reuse a nest for subsequent broods. There are usually two or more broods a year, depending on geographic location.

The pair take turns sitting on the nest during the 13–14-day incubation period.

Two pure-white eggs are laid on subsequent days (sometimes three, rarely four), followed by 13–14 days of incubation by the pair. The adults take turns on the nest, with the female sitting at night and the male relieving her at about 8 A.M. and remaining on the eggs until she returns in the late afternoon.

It is during this incubation period that a great many dove nests are destroyed. Perhaps the greatest culprit is weather. We are always amazed at how early each spring the mourning doves in our area build their first nest and lay eggs. So often, that first nest is destroyed by late spring storms, either by high winds or by ice, snow or sleet. A recent study at Texas A & M University revealed that a heavy spring rain not only wiped out most of the nests in the area, but even killed some of the incubating adults which died from exposure right on their nests.

Nests are also susceptible to predation from squirrels, cats, snakes, raccoons, and even other birds, such as blue jays and crows. Unlike some songbirds, such as robins and mockingbirds, adult mourning doves do not aggressively protect their nests and nestlings. There is one record, however, of a fledgling robin coming too close to a mourning dove nest. The male dove knocked the fledgling to the ground and smothered it to death. This has to be an exceptional act, considering the quiet personality of the dove.

This newly hatched youngster is helpless and will require constant care by both parents.

Mourning doves feed their young by regurgitating a granular fluid called "pigeon milk" into the mouths of the youngsters, as shown in this rare picture.

YOUNG WIN NO BEAUTY PRIZE

The newly hatched young, among the ugliest of all baby birds, are helpless and require the constant care of both adults. The same study at Texas A & M showed that if one adult is killed while the young are less than six days old, they, too, will die, because it takes the care of both parents to maintain the health of nestlings of that tender age.

This may be because the feeding process is so unusual, almost bizarre. Both parents regurgitate a glandular fluid called "pigeon milk," produced in their crops from the seeds they have eaten. Each youngster takes its place at the side of the feeding parent and pushes its bill inside the bill of the adult. In this position, the older bird actually pumps the pigeon milk into the mouths of the nestlings for about a minute. The process is repeated, with 5–10-second pauses,

By the time they're three days old, mourning dove squabs still have their egg teeth, but have started to grow feather quills.

The young grow rapidly, and by their 10th day, they're capable of leaving the nest. Most, however, fledge at 14 days.

until both young are full. The entire feeding process takes about six minutes. This method of feeding young by the dove/pigeon family is unique in the bird world and is strangely similar to breast-feeding among mammals.

The young, known as "squabs," are fat and unattractive, covered at first with a short white down through which their yellow skins show. Black bills and sealed black eyelids seem to add to their ugliness. As they grow, feather quills begin to show. Their new spiny plumage does nothing to enhance their appearance.

The young grow rapidly, however, and at about 10 days they are capable of leaving the nest, though 14 days is the usual age for fledging. At this time, the parent birds, though still caring for their offspring, start the nesting cycle all over again.

THE SHARE-A-NEST PLAN

There are some interesting records of mourning doves sharing nests with other species of birds. In Pennsylvania, for example, there were two robin eggs and two dove eggs in the same nest. The two females took turns incubating. Though the eggs hatched, the young lived for only eight days. There is another record of a black-billed cuckoo and a mourning dove sitting together on a robin's nest. Eggs in the nest included two of the cuckoo, two of the dove and one of the robin. Apparently the robin had not quite finished building the nest when the cuckoo took possession of it and filled it full of rootlets. However, the robin returned long enough to lay one egg.

Even when the nesting cycle is normal, most young do not survive. The death of baby doves is common; 75 percent never live through their first year. A three-year-old is considered an old bird, though there are records of some mourning doves living 10 years in the wild and 17 in captivity. One mourning dove banded in Ohio was found seven years later in Mexico.

HUNTING NOT A VILLAIN

The doves' high mortality rate cannot be blamed on hunting. Research has shown time and time again that the 12 percent that fall to the gun have no significant effect on population dynamics. That is the rationale of the 34 state conservation departments which conduct an annual dove-hunting season. In fact, the latest census figures show that mourning dove populations are actually up in the regions where the birds are hunted, and down where they are not hunted. This may reflect the law of natural compensation, where higher mortality rates cause organisms to produce more offspring.

Nor is a lack of food the cause of the high mortality rate among doves. In fact, there is a surplus of the kinds of grains that mourning doves like to eat. With the advent of mechanical harvesting equipment, the amount of waste grain left in the fields greatly increased.

Only one day out of the nest, this fledgling is still under its parents' care, even though the adults have already begun another nesting cycle.

In other words, doves never had it so good, because 98 percent of their diet consists of weed seeds and grass seeds; grains such as wheat, corn, oats, barley, buckwheat and millet; peanuts, cowpeas and lespedezas; and seeds of pines, doveweed and pokeberry. They also consume some insects, snails and grit from roadside gravel. Water is very important to doves and they may fly great distances, particularly in desert country, to drink.

Often victims of severe weather or predation, most young mourning doves do not survive.

Adults are also sensitive to severe weather conditions and often succumb to ice storms, blizzards and extended wet periods.

HIGH MORTALITY FROM MANY CAUSES

If neither hunting nor a lack of food is the primary cause of the high mortality rate among mourning doves, then what is? Actually, it is a combination of many factors, which include disease, parasites, predation, and, of course, weather. Like dove nestlings, adults are also sensitive to severe weather conditions and easily succumb to ice storms, blizzards, extended periods of wet weather, drought and heat. But as with all species, the doves' high productivity compensates for the high mortality. Most pairs produce at least two broods of two squabs each. In some areas of the country, as many as five broods are not unusual. In the Deep South, where the growing season is long, there are records of doves nesting during every month of the year.

WINTER IS A TIME FOR SOCIALIZING

Those mourning doves that nest north of the freeze line tend to behave differently than their southern or tropical kin. Following the nesting season, northern families join into small flocks and in some areas into larger flocks of hundreds of birds. Those loosely knit social groups spend the cold months together, either roving around their breeding areas or flying south to more temperate lands where food is plentiful.

In our backyard, we suspect that we are seeing two groups of doves each fall: local birds that have nested in the area and probably will stay with us through the winter, and migratory birds that have nested farther north and are headed south. During some harsh winters, I suspect that all doves in our region are somewhat migratory.

The massing of mourning doves provides some spectacular flocks of birds. During fall and winter months, they feed together in grain fields, drink together at water holes and roost together in stands of evergreens. Flights of doves to and from these massing areas are reminiscent of the heyday of the passenger pigeon.

MOURNING DOVES GRACE MANY BACKYARDS

As with all wildlife, the three needs that have to be filled in order to attract mourning doves to the backyard are food, water and cover.

Food and water are the easiest to provide. Mourning doves love cracked corn and will readily accept it at backyard feeding stations. Because they are ground feeders, the cracked corn should be placed either on the ground or on a tray feeder close to the ground. The doves at our feeders love the large, homemade tray feeders that I have nailed to stumps. Several doves will feed on the trays at one time while others scavenge for cast-off grain on the ground around the base of the feeders.

Doves will also come to backyard birdbaths. As mentioned earlier, water is very important to the dove/pigeon family and the birds will fly great distances to obtain it. Any birdbath will do, but moving or dripping water will attract more birds than still water.

Finally, there needs to be cover, probably the most important of the three basic needs. Mourning doves are easily spooked, and unless there is enough natural cover to give them a feeling of security in your backyard, they probably will not risk a visit. That means that the more trees, especially conifers, shrubs and other plants, you provide in your backyard, the more doves and other species of birds you are likely to attract. With adequate cover, doves will have escape routes through which they can retreat if or when predators appear. They can also eat in safety and possibly even build nests in the same plant materials that provide the security.

THE MOURNING DOVE HAS RELATIVES

A number of other members of the dove/pigeon family are a part of backyard bird communities across America. Undoubtedly, the most common is the barnyard or city variety of pigeon, properly called the rock dove. Larger and heavier than the mourning dove and occurring in a variety of plumage colorations from gray to fawn to white, this North African/Middle Eastern species was introduced into North America in the 1600s and has thrived. Supposedly the first bird to be domesticated, this species is raised for racing, as a carrier bird, for show and for food. Unfortunately, it has become a dirty pest in the cities and parks of this and other countries around the world. It is also a pest at many backyard feeding stations.

Conversely, the native pigeons of North America are shy, scarce and difficult to attract to backyards. They include the band-tailed pigeon of the Far West, the red-billed pigeon of the Rio Grande Valley, and the white-crowned pigeon of the Florida Keys.

There are several species of native doves that are quite common, widely distributed and frequent visitors to backyards. The white-winged dove of the Southwest is the one most like the mourning dove in both appearance and habits. The obvious difference is its flashy white wing patches which show while the bird is perching and are even more conspicuous in flight. The whitewing also has white

Water is very important to all doves, and they can be lured to backyards which provide it.

The white-winged dove of the Southwest is much like the mourning dove in both appearance and habits.

square blocks on the outer edges of its tail. Whitewings and mourning doves live together within the whitewing's southwestern range.

The remaining two native doves of North America are only about half the size of the mourning dove and not much larger than a sparrow. The common ground dove is a familiar bird from South Carolina and Georgia across the Gulf states to Texas and southern California. The Inca dove is a close relative of the common ground dove but lives only in the desert areas of the Southwest. As their family name indicates, the ground doves spend most of their time on or near the ground. Both have rusty-colored wing feathers seen only in flight.

G. H. H.

MOURNING DOVE FACTS

Description: A 12-inch brown pigeonlike bird that is larger than a robin, but smaller and slimmer than a barnyard or city pigeon (rock dove). Has long pointed tail with white edges conspicuous in flight. Sexes similar.

Habitat: Many habitats including open woods, evergreen plantations, orchards, shelterbelts, farmlands, roadside trees and suburban yards and gardens.

Nest and Eggs: Commonly in an evergreen, 10–25 feet above the ground on a horizontal branch. Loose, bulky platform of sticks. Typically 2 pure-white eggs per nesting; 2–5 broods per pair.

Food: Diet is 98 percent seeds and plant materials. Prefers cracked corn at the feeding station.

Life Span: If bird is among the 30 percent which survive the first year, may live 2–5 years in the wild. A mourning dove banded in Ohio was shot in Mexico when 7 years old. Another banded in Cape Cod lived 10 years in the wild. Two in captivity lived past 17.

Song: Coo consists of 5–7 notes: *coo-ah, cooo, cooo, coo.*

So hooked are goldfinches on Niger seed that they can be enticed to almost any object—a camera in this case—to satisfy their craving.

CHAPTER SIX

American Goldfinch—
Last Bird of Summer

Some people wait until they see the heads of skunk cabbage peering through the marsh floor or hear the robin's song to admit that spring is on its way. Weary of winter within weeks after it arrives, George and I start searching for signs long before that.

Our first signal that spring will eventually break through the somber, gray days of winter is the reappearance of bright yellow feathers here and there on our resident male goldfinches. One winter, we saw a dash of color on two of our males the week before Christmas. Usually it's just a dot on the throat or on the back of the neck, but slowly, those specks will have become splotches of sunny lemon, giving the birds' olive-colored winter garb a thoroughly mottled appearance.

By the first of May, the male is fully dressed in his brilliant yellow breeding attire, strikingly accented by jet-black wings, tail and forehead patch that is placed like a jaunty cadet's cap. He looks and sounds much like a canary, so is often misnamed "wild canary."

The female, on the other hand, doesn't look much different from the way she did during the winter. She is dull olive with dark wings that sport two conspicuous white bars. She has no cap on her dainty head.

The goldfinch is a small bird, only 4½ to 5½ inches long, and weighs just ⅓–½ ounce. Small though it is, it has a beautiful voice. Whether in full song, in conversational chatter, sounding an alarm, or as a nestling begging for food, its notes are always sweet, never harsh.

Even on the wing, the goldfinch calls out cheery phrases. Its flight is deeply undulating, so that watching a flying goldfinch is like watching a bouncing yellow ball. As it reaches the crest of each bounce, we hear a burst of *per-chik-o-ree*. It's as though the bird is exclaiming, *"Just look at me!"*

They seem to be lighthearted creatures. As Roger Tory Peterson said, "The responsibilities of life seem to rest lightly on the goldfinch's sunny shoulders." Except at the beginning of their nesting cycle, goldfinches are sociable birds, enjoying the company of others of their kind. "When we come on a lone goldfinch, it seems out of its element," Winsor Tyler commented. "It gives a long, sweet call and appears to look about for companions or to listen for them, and when it sees them or hears their voices in the distance, it goes bounding away to join them."

Artist-ornithologist George Sutton said that when he was mist-netting birds, he often had goldfinches fly deliberately into a net near a bird that was already caught and calling. With the snared birds crying plaintively, others flew into the net by twos. One time, he had twelve goldfinches to untangle at once.

BIRD OF THE OPEN COUNTRY

The goldfinch is primarily a bird of the open areas, preferring to live in orchards, in groves, along roadsides and in swamps rather than in forests. Like the mourning dove, it is a species that has actually increased its numbers as a result of man's effect on the landscape. As settlers spread westward, clearing woodlands as they went, they created expanses of open areas which later grew shrubs and small trees that the goldfinch found to its liking. Man also created goldfinch habitat in the form of fencerows, hedgerows along

Goldfinches have two distinctly different seasonal plumages. In spring, males are bright canary-yellow with black wings and cap.

In winter, goldfinches look so different in their drab plumage that many people don't believe they're the same bird.

roadways, abandoned pastures and orchards. As a result, the American goldfinch, *Carduelis tristis,* is common coast to coast, from southern Canada to the Gulf states.

THE CHORUS BEGINS IN SPRING

We have goldfinches at our bird feeders all winter, but they aren't all necessarily the same birds that lived in the area during the breeding season. Some surely are permanent residents, nesting in one of our maple trees in late summer, but others merely winter here from more northern breeding grounds.

In April, we see an influx of goldfinches as those that spent the drab winter months in more southern locales return to their summer quarters to breed. But they're in no hurry to take on family responsibilities. Still not completely outfitted in their nuptial attire, they frolic about in carefree flocks, feeding together in overgrown fields and staging melodious songfests in trees—the first stage of courtship.

"All the goldfinches of a neighborhood collect together and hold a sort of musical festival," was the way naturalist John Burroughs described it. "Many dozens may be seen in some large tree, all singing and calling in the most joyous and vivacious manner. The males sing, and the females chirp and call," he said. "The best of feeling seems to pervade the company; there is no sign of quarreling or fighting . . . and the matches seem actually to be made during these musical picnics." Nothing seems to dampen their spirits, even consecutive days of cold rains. "Bedraggled, but ardent and happy, the birds were not to be dispersed by wind or weather," Burroughs reported.

At these times, a male may take to the sky, making wide circles and dipping as much as 20 or 30 feet between the peaks of his bouncing pattern. After nesting sites are established in midsummer, the male's circling flight often follows a rough outline of his territory.

GOLDFINCHES AND THISTLES GO TOGETHER

For most wild creatures, thistledown on the wind ushers in the finale of summer and the end of the breeding season. For the goldfinch, however, it is the signal to begin housekeeping.

In late July and early August, when the gawky youngsters of other songbirds are exploring shrubbery and taking their first dip in the birdbath, the goldfinch finally gets serious about raising a family. It's no wonder the goldfinch has earned the reputation of being the last bird of summer to nest.

The flocks break up into mated pairs and nesting territories are established two weeks or more before nesting actually begins. These plots encompass at least a few trees, but sometimes may cover an area as large as 100 feet by 50 feet.

The female decides where the nest will be, choosing a site 1 to 33

Orchards, groves, swamps and suburban gardens, rather than forests, are the goldfinch's preferred habitats.

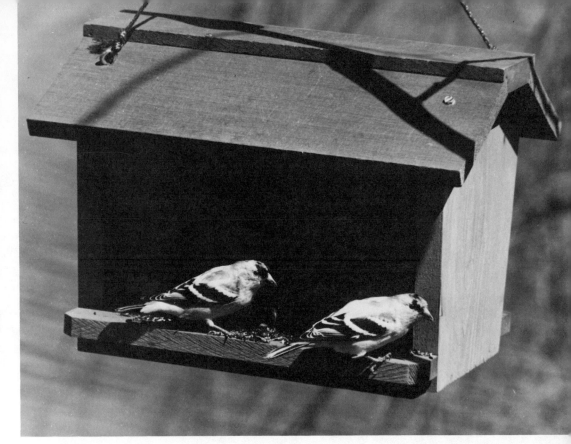

Still not completely outfitted in their nuptial attire, goldfinches spend the spring roaming in carefree flocks.

feet, but usually between 4 and 14 feet, off the ground, in a tree or shrub. It could be located anywhere within the territory.

She builds the dainty nest herself, fastening it to about four twigs to give it support. Varied plant materials are used in the construction, starting with an outer basket of stem fibers or short pieces stripped from dead branches of hawthorn, milkweed or chicory. The lining is a cozy comforter usually woven of silky thistledown, cottonwood fluff or cattail fuzz. The top is sturdily rimmed with a band of strong fibers held together with spider silk and caterpillar webs. The female works very deliberately, not rushing the project, and completes the nest in four to five days.

The finished structure is strong and durable, and so tightly woven that it will actually hold water. Some claim that baby goldfinches have drowned in water accumulated in the nest after a heavy rain,

Thistledown on the wind is the signal for goldfinches to finally get serious about raising a family.

The female chooses the nest site, which may be as high as 33 feet above the ground, as this photographer discovered.

but no one seems to have actually seen this happen. For one thing, goldfinches nest so late in the season that there is usually a full canopy of leaves sheltering the nest from all but the heaviest cloud-bursts. And, if the youngsters were so small as to be vulnerable to drowning in ½ inch or so of water, the female would undoubtedly be brooding them through the downpour.

A PATIENT SITTER

The task of nest building completed, the female may rest for about two days before laying her first egg. Painter-ornithologist Dr. George Miksch Sutton found, however, that the rest period may last as long as 27 days, and during that time the pair seem so uninterested in the nest that one might easily assume they have abandoned it.

Lined with cozy thistledown, the nest usually holds five pale bluish-white eggs.

When the female goldfinch starts laying eggs, she will produce four to six, commonly five. They are oval in shape, pale bluish-white in coloring, and unmarked.

Once she begins incubating the eggs, she is one of the most patient, diligent sitters in the bird world. The male does not help to incubate, but he feeds her during her 12–14-day stint, so she rarely leaves the nest. "During my nine hours of watching, the male goldfinch gave his mate seven substantial meals," reported ornithologist Winsor Tyler. "She took only three brief recesses from the task of incubation, totaling 25 minutes. She kept her eggs covered 95.4 percent of the time. Of ten other species of finches that I have watched incubate," he said, "none has approached the goldfinch in constancy of sitting.

"For food she depends largely upon her mate throughout the period of incubation," he continued. "She distinguishes him, evidently by voice, from other male goldfinches who fly about the vicinity dropping their little silver coins of sound; and when she hears her partner and is hungry, she calls out from the nest to attract his attention. Her clear, tinkling little notes are so sweetly melodious that one not well acquainted with the goldfinch might suppose them to be the bird's song."

Even during the intense heat of a late-summer's day, when the sun might filter through the leafy canopy to shine directly on the petite bird and her nest, she stays put. She merely turns on her own form of air conditioning—she pants, bill open, tongue extended slightly.

FRIENDLY TO ALL

The goldfinch is amazingly tolerant of intruders in its breeding territory. Other species, like towhees, cedar waxwings, thrashers and orioles, often nest congenially within the same territory.

At the beginning of their nesting cycle, goldfinches seem to be somewhat feisty about interlopers of their own kind, and occasionally there are fights between males. But as the days wear on, there is less and less territorial defense.

Goldfinch parents feed their nestlings "gold-finch porridge," partly digested seeds that are regurgitated into the babies' throats.

Conditioned to the color of their parents' feathers, these youngsters responded by begging for food when a sprig of goldenrod was held over their nest.

A DIET OF THISTLE PORRIDGE

When there are five or more eggs in the nest, which is typical of goldfinches, the young will hatch at different times over a period of about three days. It's not common, but there have been instances of goldfinch eggs producing twins.

It's hard to believe that such lovely parents can produce such ugly babies, but that is typical of many birds. The newly hatched goldfinches are covered with light-gray down and their eyes are tightly sealed. Yet, by the second or third day, they see the first rays of light as their eyes begin to open.

The youngsters are quiet, making little or no noise for nearly a week. Then, they are like our own babies when they realize that they can make sounds—they love to hear themselves. When their

Even when busy with nesting responsibilities, our goldfinches still manage to drop in several times a day for a quick snack of Niger seed.

Sunflower seed is another goldfinch favorite, almost as popular as Niger.

parents return to the nest to feed them, they tend to get quite noisy in their excitement.

Food for goldfinch babies is different from what is given to most nestlings. Usually, parent birds feed a high-protein diet of insects or worms to their young while they are in the nest. Goldfinches give their youngsters what might be called "goldfinch porridge." It's actually seeds—mostly from thistles—that have been specially prepared for the young birds.

"I have never found the nest of a goldfinch very far from an adequate supply of thistle seed," claimed W. P. Nickell, who studied goldfinches for a number of years.

The adults crack and discard the hulls and fill up on the seeds. Back at the nest, they regurgitate the partly digested seeds as "cereal" into the throats of their nestlings, one nestling at a time. The male goldfinch used this same technique to feed his mate during the incubation period.

On this diet, the young birds develop quickly. By the time they are 10 days old, feathers are beginning to grow, giving the babies enough cover so they no longer need to be brooded overnight. Snuggled together in the nest cup, the young birds keep each other warm with their body heat while the female spends the night in nearby branches.

At the age of about 12 days, the nestlings have grown so big that they exceed the capacity of their nest cup. They literally overflow, and the time for them to make their first flight is probably only a day or two away.

By now, the parents have gotten a little lax in their housekeeping. When the nestlings were smaller, the adults were very conscientious about removing fecal sacs (droppings) from the nest. Now that the youngsters are older and much larger, the adults have a hard time

Famous for their attraction to tubular feeders, goldfinches will also use natural feeders such as this split log.

Goldfinches will flock to Niger-filled sock feeders, but squirrels can easily gnaw through the nylon mesh.

being fastidious. In order to keep from fouling the nest, the young birds perch on the rim and let their droppings fall over the edge, but they often adhere to the structure. This is one of the ways to identify a goldfinch nest. The outside is thickly rimmed with their excrement, something that strikes me as being quite out of character for this otherwise tidy bird.

FIRST FLIGHT IS NOT SPECTACULAR

When the time comes for the young to leave the nest, those that hatched first will naturally be stronger and more capable than their younger brothers and sisters. Yet, all in the nest usually make their first flight on the same day.

One baby bird will climb out of the nest and make its way up an adjoining branch. Then another follows, and another, until all not only have left the nest behind, but also have attempted short flights from branch to branch. The older ones might fly 50 yards or more; the younger ones might do little more than flutter to the ground.

Once out of the nest, the youngsters are still dependent on their parents to feed them for several more weeks until they learn to find seeds themselves.

Goldfinches are among the most frequent drinkers and bathers at the recirculating garden pool.

As they become more adventurous in their eating habits, they will also eat a few insects, including small caterpillars, grasshoppers, aphids and beetles. But primarily, goldfinches eat seeds, particularly those of the composite plants like thistle and dandelion. In fact, goldfinches love dandelion seeds so much that they can barely wait for the flowers to ripen to the fuzzy white "Santa Claus" stage. We've seen them pull out the immature seeds when the flowers are still golden.

When the young master their flight skills, the family joins others in cheery bands to roam the countryside. Many move southward in flocks that advance a little each day; others stay behind to spend the winter in the North.

IS THAT THE SAME BIRD?

Beginning in September, the birds go through a complete molt. Olive drab is the autumn and winter fashion for all goldfinches, male and female, immature and adult. Juvenile males and females retain a drab plumage like their mother's throughout the autumn and winter. By October, even the adult males begin to look like females as the autumn molt passes. In most cases, their dapper black caps completely disappear, and their canary-yellow feathers are gradually replaced by olive ones. In preparation for the cold days ahead, nature is covering each bird's body with about 1,000 more feathers than it had during the summer.

By late November, all goldfinches appear pretty much alike, but by looking closely, we can see that the wings of the adult males are blacker than those of their female and immature companions.

Several times, people who have been at our home and seen the goldfinches at our bird feeders at this time of the year ask what kind of birds they are. "No, those can't be goldfinches!" they insist, remembering the brilliant yellow-and-black of the summer males.

GETTING A GOOD NIGHT'S SLEEP

Foraging across the winter landscape in their little flocks or visiting our bird feeders, goldfinches are always in each other's company. Only at night might they be alone as they roost, perhaps in the shelter of a dense evergreen, seemingly undaunted by the cold.

Overnight shelters aren't always the same, and the birds have to

By late November, all goldfinches look very much alike, but the wings of the adult males are blacker than those of females and juveniles.

Undaunted by winter's cold, goldfinches are steady customers at most northern feeding stations.

make do with what they can find. Many years ago, Dr. Charles Townsend recalled an anecdote about a New England goldfinch he had seen trying to find shelter for the night. "At sunset of a winter's day, late in January, I found one of these birds anxiously flitting about a small pine grove, alighting at the bases of trees, and finally popping into a hole about a foot deep in the snow under a stump," he wrote. "Frightened from there, it flew about nervously for a few minutes, but at last returned to the same hole close beside which I was sitting motionless. As it was now nearly dark, I had not been sure of the bird's identity, so I tried to catch it in my hat but it escaped," Townsend admitted. "The bird finally cuddled into the protected side of a footprint in the snow. It was evident that the goldfinch had been searching for a protected hole in which to pass the night—a safe place in that region as the snow showed no mark of prowling animals,'' he remarked.

NIGER SEED IS FOOLPROOF

On most winter days, I can look out my window to see dozens of goldfinches fluttering around feeders hanging against a snowy backdrop. My amiable little olive companions are even-tempered and polite (unless they are competing for a prime perch on the Niger seed feeder), and the gentle sound of their *swee-swee* is indeed welcome.

Anyone who has provided Niger seed (a tiny black import erroneously named ''thistle seed'') at a feeding station knows that it works like a goldfinch magnet. Once these birds discover a ready supply of Niger at your feeder, they will stay with you well into the summer, becoming less visible for only a few weeks to satisfy their breeding instincts. Then they are back. We find that even when they are busy with domestic chores, they still manage to sneak in once or twice a day for a quick snack of Niger seed. This is either out of habit or because they really love it, for natural food, particularly the wild thistle, is plentiful. I wouldn't be surprised if the goldfinch babies in our maple tree were raised on Niger seed porridge.

Niger seed is more expensive than other types of bird seed, but the ''black gold'' is worth it. Not only do the goldfinches get hooked on it, but you'll find that it also draws purple finches, house finches, pine siskins and redpolls.

Sunflower seed is another goldfinch favorite, almost as popular as Niger.

In the warmer months, water is particularly enticing to the goldfinches. They probably drink and bathe more often at our patio pools than any other species, with the possible exception of the robins.

Cover, too, is important for the birds to feel comfortable in your backyard. Thickets, hedges, clumps of shrubbery, and shade trees will help them feel at home.

One of the goldfinch's relatives is the purple finch. The male of the species looks like it's been dipped in raspberry juice.

A FAMILY OF COLORFUL COUSINS

The American goldfinch is one of a colorful family. Close relatives include the lesser goldfinch, *Carduelis psaltria,* found abundantly in some areas of the West, as far north as southwestern Washington state, and as far south as northern South America. Another western species, Lawrence's goldfinch, *Carduelis lawrencei,* is recognized by its black face, gray head and yellow wing bars. It breeds in California and winters as far east as western Texas.

Others in the family Fringillidae are the finches that look like they've been dipped in raspberry juice. The purple finch, *Carpodacus purpureus,* is a northern bird that is common at backyard feeders and winters as far south as northern Mexico. It closely resembles the slightly brighter house finch, *Carpodacus mexicanus,* basically a western bird ranging from British Columbia to Mexico, but rapidly expanding its range in the East, and the somewhat paler Cassin's finch, *Carpodacus cassinii,* fairly common in the West from British Columbia to central Mexico. The females of these three species are streaked brown.

K. P. H.

AMERICAN GOLDFINCH FACTS

Description: A small olive-yellow bird with white bars on dark wings. In spring, male's plumage changes to bright canary-yellow with jet-black wings, tail and forehead patch. Bouncing flight is often punctuated with the *per-chik-o-ree* call as the bird reaches the peak of a bounce and begins the downward swoop.

Habitat: Open country, especially shrubby roadsides, orchards, groves, fencerows and swamps.

Nest and Eggs: Tightly woven cup of plant fibers and grasses, often lined with thistledown or cattail down. From 4 to 6, but usually 5, pale, bluish-white eggs.

Food: Mostly seeds. Especially fond of wild thistle and dandelion seeds. Enjoys Niger and sunflower seeds at bird feeders. Also eats some insects, especially in spring.

Life Span: Probably about 3 years, if it lives to adulthood. Records of banded birds show that a few lived to be 6–8 years old. One captive bird lived to be at least 12 years old, another 13.

Song: Sweet, clear, high-pitched canarylike melody.

State Bird: Iowa, New Jersey and Washington.

After spending the winter alone, the male downy seems to come to life in early February.

CHAPTER SEVEN

Downy Woodpecker— A Friendly Jackhammer

It's January. The woods are silent, except for a solitary *tap, tap, tap! Tap, tap, tap!* It's not a loud tap, but it is distinct. It's a welcome sound amid the stillness of a snow-laden world.

Searching the dark skeletons of dormant oaks, I spot the little black-and-white mite. It's a downy woodpecker, the smallest of its clan. On closer examination, I see that it's a male, for only the male downy has a red spot on the back of its head.

Tap, tap tap! Tap, tap, tap! The bird is all alone, for the downy is solitary in winter. It will follow chickadees, titmice and nuthatches around, but it doesn't associate with its own kind until early spring.

Tap, tap, tap! Tap, tap, tap! Interesting how it props itself with those stiff tail feathers while clinging to the bark. The tail relieves the toes of the bird's weight. This unique tripod allows the downy to hop up the tree trunk with ease, but it must back down in the same position, a more awkward motion. Its pincerlike feet are also unique. Most birds have three toes in the front of the foot and one in the back. But the woodpeckers have adapted to their needs with two toes in the front and two in the back. This gives them a better

The downy's tripod—stiff tail feathers and two pincerlike feet —allows the bird to hitch up the tree trunk with ease.

Wooded backyards, like this one, could host a family of downy woodpeckers.

grasp on the bark. Like most woodpeckers, the downy's outer hind toe is longer to keep the bird from swaying.

Tap, tap, tap! Tap, tap, tap! That bill, too, is special. It is chisel-shaped, not pointed as on most other birds. They need that flat chisel tip for carving their nesting and roosting cavities. They also need it to chip away the wood around the insects buried in tree trunks. Once they chisel close to the morsel, their amazing tongue does the rest of the work. Surprisingly long and sticky, twice the length of the bird's head, it has a horny tip of recurved barbs used to spear the borers.

That little jackhammer bill also requires a very special skull behind it. Not only is it a stronger and thicker skull than other kinds of birds have, but it is also heavier. The added weight makes the hammer more effective.

OUR SMALLEST WOODPECKER

The tapping sound gives the impression that the downy woodpecker, *Picoides pubescens,* is larger than six inches, but the smallest woodpecker in North America is actually not as big as a robin. It's about the size of a sparrow. It can be separated from all other woodpeckers—except the hairy—by the broad, white strip down its back. A black-and-white miniature of the hairy woodpecker, the downy is two-thirds the size of the hairy, with a smaller, stubbier bill. The females of both species lack the red spot on the back of their heads. Both get their names from the short, soft feathers around their nostrils.

Like other members of the woodpecker clan, the downy has a distinct undulating flight that is most evident when it crosses open areas or swoops through woodlands. The dips are not as deep as those of a goldfinch, but as ornithologist Arthur Cleveland Bent said, "It gives the effect of a ship pitching slightly in a heavy sea. A few strokes carry the bird up to the crest of the wave—the wings clapping close to the side of the body—then, at the crest, with the wings shut, the bird tilts slightly forward, and slides down into the next trough."

The downy is also our friendliest woodpecker. At our feeding station, it will back down to the suet container on the basswood tree while we sit only a few feet away on the patio. Even when we walk right up to them, most downies will not fly, but will simply scoot around the backside of the tree trunk and then peek around to see what we are doing. If we press them, they will hop up the backside of the tree trunk and then fly to a higher branch.

When European settlers invaded the downy woodpeckers' territory 200 to 300 years ago, the birds did not retreat as did many of our native species. Instead, they accepted as a home the orchards and shade trees with which man replaced the forests. Our early ornithologists were in agreement when they characterized the bird. Audubon remarked in 1842 that it "is perhaps not surpassed by any of its tribe in hardiness, industry, or vivacity." Alexander Wilson said 10 years earlier that "the principal characteristics of this little

Courtship begins with a curious weaving action by both sexes, accompanied by considerable chattering.

bird are diligence, familiarity, perseverance,'' and spoke of a pair of downies working at their nest ''with the most indefatigable diligence.'' And so it is today. The downy woodpecker remains unspoiled and unconcerned by the threats of man. It just quietly flits around the backyard woodland, *tap, tap tap*-ping its way through life.

Downy woodpeckers inhabit most of the wooded areas of North America, except the deserts. They are not a deep-forest bird either, preferring open woodlands, river groves, orchards, swamps, farmlands and suburban backyards. They have been recorded nesting at elevations up to 9,000 feet.

Downies characteristically carve their nesting cavity 3–50 feet above the ground on the underside of an exposed limb.

Four to five pure-white eggs are a typical clutch for the downy woodpecker. The parents share the 12-day incubation chore.

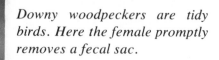

Downy woodpeckers are tidy birds. Here the female promptly removes a fecal sac.

SPRING COMES EARLY FOR THE DOWNY

Regardless of the elevation, downy woodpeckers begin thinking about nesting earlier than most birds and several months before they actually nest. After spending the winter alone, the downies seem to come to life in early February, moving more quickly and taking more interest in members of their own species. Their normal *tap, tap, tap* becomes a quite different unbroken *trrrrrrrrrrrrrrrrr*, lasting several seconds. The tapping is no longer simply an effort to find food, but a means of communicating to other downies that this is "my" territory. It is also the first attempt to attract a mate. Both sexes drum. So early does this drumming begin that it is not unusual to hear it on subzero mornings. One observer commented that the downies' "percussion sound is their contribution to the orchestration of the bird chorus."

Though drumming is the downies' song, they do make some vocal noises. They have several single-syllable call notes which include a *tchick,* an aggressive social note; a *tick* and a *tkhirrrr,* which are alarm notes. There is also a location call, known as a "whinny," made up of a dozen or more *tchicks* all strung together.

Some ornithologists believe that downy woodpeckers retain the same mate as long as they live. In this case, all the pair has to do in the spring is to renew their pair bonds. This fidelity, however, seems to be a result of an attachment to the nesting site rather than between the birds.

After the drumming has united the pair, the actual courtship begins with a curious dance or "weaving" action by both sexes. With their neck stretched out and bill pointed in line with their body, they pivot their head and body from side to side balancing on the tips of their tail. Their entire body is elongated. There is also a lot of flitting and chasing from one branch to another, and more waving and weaving of head and body, sometimes with wing and tail feathers spread. Considerable chattering accompanies these gyrations.

When two males or two females come face to face over a territorial dispute, they spread their wings, raise their crests and assume a challenging attitude and scold each other. Most of this is bluff, of course, for they soon settle down, unless one or the other advances toward a female.

Sometime during this courting period, the actual selection of a nesting cavity occurs. The female is usually, though not always, the dominant bird and selects the nesting site. Once selected, both birds dig the hole. Downies will characteristically place the nesting cavity entrance hole 3–50 feet above the ground on the underside of an exposed dead limb. The pair will alternate digging because only one bird at a time can fit into the cavity. As the hole is cut deeper, the bird working may disappear into the hole and remain out of sight for 15–20 minutes, appearing only long enough to throw out chips. (Unlike chickadees, which will carry their chips away from the nesting site, downies are not concerned about predators finding chips at the base of the nesting tree.) Then the pair will change shifts for 15 or 20 minutes while the other bird digs. Though the female does most of the work, this may vary with individual pairs. Regardless, the cavity is finished in about a week.

A GOURD-SHAPED NESTING CAVITY

When the cavity is completed, sometime in mid-May, it is shaped much like a gourd. The entrance is 1¼ inches in diameter. It is dug straight in about 4 inches, then curves down 8–10 more inches and widens to about 3 inches in diameter. At the very bottom, the cavity narrows to about 2 inches, where a few chips are left to serve as a nest. It is believed that woodpeckers have been nesting in cavities so long in evolutionary time that nesting material is no longer used. Chickadees and bluebirds have been nesting in cavities for a shorter period of time, and still build a nest at the bottom of the cavity as they did when they built their nests in the open.

The eggs, too, reflect this. Species that have been using cavities for many thousands of years, like the woodpeckers, lay pure-white eggs. No protective coloration is needed when they are hidden in a cavity. Bluebirds and chickadees, on the other hand, still lay eggs with some protective coloration on them—specks in the case of chickadees and pale blue in bluebirds' eggs.

The fluffy, or "downy," fledglings become independent and solitary at about six weeks of age.

Downy woodpeckers lay four to five pure-white eggs, which are incubated by both parents through the 12 days required for hatching. They take turns during the daylight hours; the male incubates at night.

NAKED, RED AND HOMELY

When the young hatch, they are naked, blind, helpless, red-colored and quite unattractive. During the first few critical days after hatching, the adults take turns in the cavity, one brooding the young while the other bird is gathering food. The male usually broods at night.

Downies do not swallow their food and then regurgitate it to the young as do some birds. Instead, they carry insects, primarily spiders, ants and moths, to the youngsters in their bills. The older the chicks get, the more food the adults must provide. It isn't long before the young can be heard chippering in the cavity and both parents are feeding from daylight until dark. At times they are feeding as often as once a minute!

A few days after hatching, feathers start to grow on the young, and by the time they are 14 days old, their tail feathers are long enough and strong enough to support their weight. It is then that they make their first appearance at the cavity entrance. For the next week, the youngsters spend a great deal of their time taking turns at the cavity entrance, heads out, chippering loudly, awaiting the next meal. At 21–24 days, the young are ready to leave the cavity on their first flight. A New York State observer gave a good account of a downy family's last few days in the cavity: "The young chattered most of the time during the last two days of nest life. One at a time they looked out a great deal at the strange outer world. They left the nest on June 11. The last two, a male and a female, left during the afternoon, each after being fed at the entrance and seeing the parent fly away. The young male flew from the nesting hole straight to a tree 60 feet away. His sister quickly followed, lighting on the trunk of the same tree and following her parent up the bole in the hitching manner of their kind as though she had been practicing this vertical locomotion all of her life."

The observer could distinguish male youngsters from female because they already had a slightly different appearance. Like their adult counterparts, the young males have red on their heads and the females do not. The red on the head of the juvenile male is not a small spot on the back of the head as in the adult male, but a much larger area of red and pink on the whole crown. The youngsters are also somewhat fluffy or "downy" looking. The juvenile female looks like the juvenile male, without the red crown.

This juvenal plumage will be worn but a short time, for all downies, young and adult, molt into winter plumage in September.

Once the young have fledged, the parents divide up the brood and only take care of their charges. The male will usually take one or two of the young, while the female takes the others. According to one study, young downies become independent at the age of 41 days. I can believe this, as I have seen youngsters on our suet feeders in late summer with no apparent adult escort, nor any interest in other downies in the area. In fact, I have seen adults drive off youngsters at the suet feeders.

Downy woodpeckers have only one brood a year in the North, but sometimes two in the South.

THEY EAT MANY INSECT ENEMIES

Besides being friendly, downy woodpeckers are our good friends for another reason. Most of the insects they eat are considered destructive to man's orchards and forest products. About 75 percent of their diet consists of animal matter gleaned from the bark and crevices where insect larvae and eggs lie hidden. While standing on that unique tripod of two legs and a tail, downies hitch up and down tree trunks in search of a whole laundry list of insect pests. With their special chisel-like bills and horny, sticky tongues, downies are adept at plucking out great numbers of beetle grubs, insect cocoons or batches of insect eggs. They also eat spiders, snails, berries of poison ivy, mountain ash, Virginia creeper and dogwood, and many other tree and shrub seeds, including oak, hickory and beech mast.

Dr. John Confer and his students at Ithaca College have studied the downy woodpecker's use of goldenrod galls as a source of food. They discovered that the downy's little jackhammer is just the tool needed to drill a hole in the side of the 1–2-inch goldenrod gall and extract the tiny grub contained inside. In fact, Confer's studies show that the goldenrod grubs form an important part of the woodpecker's winter diet. I have used those grubs for catching panfish through the ice for years, but didn't realize until recently that downy woodpeckers have a taste for them, too.

Downy woodpeckers drill through the walls of goldenrod galls to extract the succulent grubs housed inside.

The most popular feeding-station food for downy woodpeckers is beef suet.

REASONABLY SAFE FROM PREDATORS

Though no songbird is totally safe from predators, not many downy woodpeckers fall prey to hawks, owls and other winged hunters. When attacked, downies are quite adroit at dodging raptors by flitting around the tree trunks and branches of their natural habitat. They can also flatten themselves against the bark of a tree trunk and become almost invisible to any pursuer. Maurice Thompson described a downy's defense against a goshawk: "The downy darted through the foliage and flattened itself against a large oak bough, where it remained as motionless as the bark itself. The hawk

An inexpensive suet feeder can be made from a small log which has been drilled with one-inch-diameter holes into which the suet is stuffed.

Another homemade feeder for downies is constructed from wide-mesh hardware cloth, a plastic coffee-can lid and a wooden dowel.

Still another homemade suet feeder was fashioned out of wire coat hangers.

lit on the same bough within a few feet of its intended victim, and remained sitting there for a few moments, searching in vain. The black and white feathers of the downy blended perfectly with the bark and lichen on the tree.''

Other enemies, strangely, include house wrens, which have been known to wait until downies have completed work on their nesting cavities before appropriating the site for themselves. Unbelievable as it may sound, the house wren can be aggressive enough to attack a pair of downies and drive them from their own nesting site to procure the cavity for its own.

Squirrels, particularly red squirrels, will destroy the eggs and young of downy woodpeckers.

PREPARATIONS FOR WINTER

By September, the downy woodpecker family has broken up, the young of the year look like adults, and all become solitary and quiet.

As cold weather approaches, the first order of business is to locate a winter roosting cavity. Apparently, downies do not use their nesting cavities as winter roosts; most birds drill fresh roosts in anticipation of the long winter ahead.

These preparations, however, are not made at the fast pace of most other birds in autumn. The species that must migrate to warmer climates seem to be restless and in such a hurry about everything. But not the downy. It remains calm in the midst of the hustle. Such is the personality of the permanent resident. Despite this, there are studies which indicate that some downies, particularly females, do leave the breeding territory; others don't. The reasons for these variations are not clear.

The downy's winter is spent quietly and alone, searching the dormant woodlands for food. The pace of life has slowed, and often its *tap, tap, tap* is the only sound to be heard above the wind in the trees. The downy is well equipped to survive in the coldest weather. It even takes playful baths in snow piled high on branches. A woman in Canada described one such incident: ''This morning a female downy flew to a horizontal branch and proceeded vigorously to bathe in the loose snow lying there. Like a robin in a puddle,

A clever backyard birder satisfies this downy wood-pecker with a feeding-station food, suet, tied to a natural food, sumac.

Mrs. Downy ducked her head, ruffled her feathers and fluttered her wings, throwing some of the snow over her back and scattering the rest to the winds.''

The downy woodpecker's winter food is not unlimited. The insects upon which it survives stopped multiplying when cold weather arrived. As time passes, the bird must search more and more diligently to feed itself. It gets some help from the bands of chickadees, titmice and nuthatches with whom it shares the winter woods. Downies will often stay loosely associated with these species as they cruise the woodlands in search of hidden morsels. But the downy is also tied down somewhat to the area near its roosting hole, since it will return to it every evening at sunset. Therefore, the feeding areas surrounding the roosting cavity become a downy's individual winter feeding territory, which it will defend against other downies.

Backyard feeding stations are the exception. For some unexplained reason, feeding stations are a "common ground" for all birds in all seasons. We usually have between six and ten downies eating our suet at various times every day during the winter. We have fewer in the summer. That must be because there is more natural food available in the summer and breeding territories are more rigorously defended. Regardless, the downies do take turns at our feeders, abiding by some kind of truce at the suet, though there are often fights over who feeds first.

Bird banding records show that one downy in Minnesota lived for 12 years and 5 months.

Next to the downy, the most common backyard woodpecker is the northern flicker.

WOODED BACKYARDS ATTRACT DOWNY WOODPECKERS

Food, cover and water are the three basic needs of all wildlife and downy woodpeckers are no exception. Food and cover definitely take priority over water, as downies seldom drink at birdbaths.

Mature trees in an open woodland are the preferred habitat, but any kind of natural cover is better than none at all. We have a mixed stand of oaks, basswood, maples and willows in our yard, which suits the downies perfectly.

Food is simple. Downy woodpeckers love beef suet. Be sure that you get real beef suet at the butcher shop. So often a butcher will give or sell you beef fat, which the downies will reluctantly eat in winter. They prefer real suet, which is the white, hard, opaque fat surrounding the beef kidney. Regular beef fat has a greasier, translucent appearance. It will also decompose in warm weather and attract flies. Suet will not. That is why we recommend feeding beef suet all year long. It is every bit as successful with downies in summer as in winter. Plus, the suet feeder is the place where we first see the baby downies. Their red caps and roly-poly appearance are so cute. At first a parent bird feeds the youngster suet. Then it tries to get the youngster to feed itself. All that entertainment is ours to enjoy just because we feed suet in the summertime.

Other feeding station foods that downies will eat include peanut butter (it's a fallacy that peanut butter sticks in the throats of birds), doughnuts and an occasional sunflower seed or cracked corn kernel. But beef suet is by far the most popular with all the woodpeckers.

Will a downy woodpecker nest in a birdhouse? Though most books on attracting birds or building birdhouses give dimensions for downy woodpecker houses, there does not appear to be any record of a downy nesting in a man-made house. However, there are records of downies using birdhouses as winter roosts.

OTHER WOODPECKERS AROUND THE UNITED STATES

North America is blessed with an abundance of woodpecker species. Almost every habitat of every region of the country has its own kind of woodpeckers. There are 21 species recorded for the continent. Many are frequent visitors to backyards across the United States. There have been at least six species of woodpeckers in our own backyard in Wisconsin: besides our favorite, the downy, we regularly see hairies and occasionally red-headed and red-bellied woodpeckers, and yellow-bellied sapsuckers and flickers.

The hairy woodpecker, *Picoides villosus,* is most like the downy in appearance. Indeed, it is a carbon copy except for being half again as large as the downy and having a proportionately larger bill. You probably won't notice, but the male hairy's red spot on the back of his head is really two spots touching. On the downy, it is only one spot. Also, on close examination, the hairy's outer tail feathers are pure white, while the downy's have some black spots on them. Like the downy, the hairy is common throughout most of North America. We have at least one male and female in our yard all year. They are not as friendly, being a little more timid and wary than the downies.

The large crow-size woodpecker, the pileated, is an infrequent visitor to some backyards.

A southern species, the red-bellied woodpecker, has extended its range northward.

Probably the next most common backyard woodpecker found throughout North America is the northern flicker, *Colaptes auratus,* a rather big (slightly larger than a robin) brown woodpecker with a white rump, conspicuous black speckles on its back and a black bib in front. Males are identified by a prominent mustache (black in the East; red in the West). Flickers eat ants, and therefore spend a great deal of their time on the ground.

The red-headed woodpecker, *Melanerpes erythrocephalus,* is one of the most striking of all North American woodpeckers. Primarily an eastern species, the red-headed has an entirely red head, white belly and large white areas in its blue-black wings and back. In recent years, the redheads have made a noticeable comeback, to the point of being almost common in some open oak woodlands.

A southeastern species, the red-bellied woodpecker, *Melanerpes carolinus,* has extended its range in recent years into the upper Midwest and New England. We feel fortunate to have had this species with us in Wisconsin for the past several years. Slightly smaller than a flicker, the red-bellied has a zebralike back with a red cap and white rump. Red covers the crown and nape of the male, but only the nape of the female.

The yellow-bellied sapsucker, *Sphyrapicus varius,* completes the list of common backyard species of woodpeckers. This quiet and retiring bird has narrow wing stripes and a finely mottled back. Its yellow belly and red-and-black face markings separate it from the other woodpeckers. Sapsuckers drill orderly rows of small holes around tree trunks for sap and for the insects that are attracted to the sap.

There are quite a few other North American woodpeckers, some of which do spend time in the backyards of their regions. They include the pileated, which are the largest of our living woodpeckers; the red-cockaded, an endangered species living in the Southeast; the black-backed and the three-toed of the North and Northwest; the golden-fronted, Strickland's (formerly Arizona), ladder-backed and gila of the Southwest; the acorn woodpecker, Lewis' woodpecker, Williamson's sapsucker and red-breasted sapsucker of the Northwest; and Nuttall's and white-headed of the Far West.

G. H. H.

DOWNY WOODPECKER FACTS

Description: Smallest and most common backyard woodpecker in North America; smaller than a robin, about the size of a sparrow; white back and belly, with black-and-white markings elsewhere. Males have small red spot on back of head. Two-thirds the size, but otherwise a near carbon copy of the hairy woodpecker.

Habitat: Open forests of mixed growth, orchards, swamps, river groves and wooded backyards.

Nest and Eggs: In cavity of either live or dead tree, 3–50 feet above the ground; 4 or 5 pure-white eggs; incubation by both parents; one brood in North, sometimes two in the South.

Food: The 75 percent that is animal matter consists mostly of economically harmful insects such as beetles, wood-boring larvae, caterpillars, weevils and ants. Remainder of diet includes wild fruits, seeds and nuts. At feeding station, beef suet is the most popular food.

Life Span: If the youngster survives the first year, it will probably live an average of 5–7 years in the wild. Banding records have produced some ancient downies. One from Minnesota had lived 12 years, 5 months when recaptured. Other banding records show that 7–8 years is not unusual.

Song: The downy woodpecker's song is actually its drumming on a tree with its little jackhammer bill. However, it does have a quiet call note, which is a single, abrupt syllable, like *tchick*. Another note is a long whinny made up of a dozen or more *tchicks*.

The male house wren's sweet, bubbling song not only advertises posses-sion of his territory, but serves to attract a female as well.

CHAPTER EIGHT

House Wren— Garden Troubadour

The little house wren must surely be one of the most tenacious birds in the world when it comes to nesting. Once it decides that your yard is its home, nothing will keep it from nesting there. Ours is a classic example.

During the year we rebuilt our home, a pair of wrens laid claim to their usual summer residence—the box in the second apple tree from the garage—and got busy building their nest. On the day our basement was excavated, the wrens had just completed their own construction project and the female had probably already laid one egg.

We felt certain that they would desert their nest because of all the commotion. Not only did they stick it out to raise their brood of five spunky youngsters, but they persevered to bring off a second brood in the same box. They held out in spite of steam shovels, front-end loaders, cement mixers; even in spite of having a big dump truck parked only inches below their nest for most of the season. During the second nesting, our septic system was replaced. The digging for the new one came within six feet of the wrens' apple tree. In addition, four large trees had to be removed, and a small outbuilding relocated, all within 20 yards of the wrens' nursery.

Any other songbird I can think of would have hightailed it out of there by the second day of disruption, if not on the first. Yet, the wrens stubbornly clung to their homestead, coming and going so discreetly that most of the workmen on the job were unaware of their presence.

That tenacity is part of the wren's charm. It also makes the house wren, within most of its range, one of the easiest birds to entice to a nesting box in your garden. This, combined with an effervescent, joyous song, is why the wren is a favorite among backyard birders.

Our house wren is sometimes called the jenny wren, a nickname given to it by English settlers who were reminded of the little wren of their homeland.

A LITTLE BROWN BUNDLE OF ENERGY

Wrens are drab brown birds that are always busy, busy, busy. The house wren, *Troglodytes aedon,* is the plainest and commonest, lacking the facial striping of some other wrens. They are jaunty little birds, with short, upcocked tails. They measure less than five inches in length and weigh only a few grams—probably about ⅓ ounce. Their most distinguishing characteristic is their song—an absolute joy to hear. I think it's downright impossible to feel gloomy when a wren is singing outside your window.

Tiny though it is, the wren has a volatile temper and aggressively attacks other birds—and larger intruders—that it feels are invading its territory. Restless and curious, it will usually come to investigate if you "squeak" it in with loud kisses on the back of your hand.

House wrens like open woodlands, parks and shrubby areas, and are obviously quite fond of suburban backyards.

No doubt this was why the Cherokee Indians thought of the wren as a busybody. According to their legends, the wren awakened at dawn to make the rounds of every lodge, gathering tidbits of information to pass along to the "birds' council." A Cherokee birth was always a newsworthy event, but if the wren announced that the baby was a boy, the birds were distressed. They realized that when the little boy was old enough, he would hunt them and roast them on a spit. But if the newsgatherer announced a baby girl, the wrens were delighted. In a few years, the girl would learn to make cornmeal. Some would be spilled, providing a bit of food for the wrens.

Folklore such as this leads us to believe that wrens have always lived close to humans.

Today, house wrens still live in harmony with humans from southern Canada to Argentina, breeding from southern British Columbia to Maine, and as far south as Texas and Georgia. They prefer open woodlands, parks, and shrubby areas, and are obviously quite fond of suburban backyards.

THE MERRY MONTH OF MAY MEANS WRENS

We're aware of the first wren of the season when the male arrives to stake out his territory in our backyard in late April or early May. He sings constantly, almost mechanically, during this period, both to advertise his possession of an area from ¼ to 3½ acres and to attract a female. Besides singing to announce that the territory already has a tenant, the male scolds, threatens, chases, and, if necessary, fights intruders off his turf.

While he waits for the females to arrive about a fortnight later, the male busies himself with housework. He is a compulsive nest starter, stuffing any possible nest site with coarse twigs and similar material. It's not unusual to find a half dozen of these "dummy" nests on a wren's territory. There seem to be two reasons for his doing this. One is that it tells other birds, especially other wrens, that there is no vacancy at that site. The other reason is that it is part of the courtship ritual for the male to take his mate on a tour of all these crude stick nests so that she may decide which location, if any, suits her.

A male wren will fill up every available nesting site in his territory with "dummy" nests.

A FERVENT SUITOR

We can usually tell when the females arrive just by the change in the male's song. Though it's basically the same, he really throws himself into it, producing an even sweeter, bubblier, rippling song. It's clear why the Chippewa Indians named this little bird *O-du-na-mis-sug-ud-da-we'-shi,* "a big noise for its size." The song has been called an almost nonstop burst of melody—loud, hurried, strenuous, ecstatic and difficult to describe or to translate into written words.

Besides the change in song, we see a change in the male's general deportment, too. Before there were females to sing to, the male kept his saucy tail lowered. But now, excited by the presence of a possible mate, he wears his tail tilted upward as he delivers his courtship song. The more excited he becomes, the farther forward his tail tilts!

The male wren courts his lady ardently, and with much bustling the pair inspect all the dummy nests he built over the last week or two. Cocking their short tails upward, their wings quivering with excitement, they flit from one nest possibility to another.

QUAINT NESTING HABITS

The wren's family name, Troglodytidae, is from the Greek word meaning "creeper into holes," and nearly any hole that a wren can creep into seems to be an appropriate place to build a nest. Wrens will commonly build in the wren houses that are put out for them, but they aren't fussy. As a matter of fact, they've been known to be rather eccentric in their preferences. A mailbox, a basket or a discarded rusty tin can might be their idea of the perfect honeymoon bungalow. I once saw a pair nesting in the iron pipe railing of a bridge in Pennsylvania. Hal Harrison photographed a wren nest that had been built in the leg of a pair of work pants hanging on a clothesline. The wife of the pants owner tied up the leg and relinquished the pants to the birds. Eggs were laid, and the young were raised inside, finally leaving the trousers when they fledged.

Watering pots, fishing creels, sun hats, teapots and old boots have also been chosen as nesting sites. One pair of wrens built their nest on the rear axle of a car that was used daily. When the car was driven, the wrens went along. The eggs, nevertheless, hatched successfully.

Other wrens have used deserted oriole nests hanging 20 feet above the ground, a kingfisher's nesting hole in a sandy stream bank, and the deep recesses of an osprey's nest. On an island in Virginia, 24 empty cow skulls were found bleaching in the sun. They were hung in trees and shrubbery, and almost immediately 23 of the skulls were occupied by wrens who readily accepted the gruesome houses. When it comes to house wren nests, the uncommon is fairly common.

*When the female ar-
rives on the scene,
she chooses the loca-
tion she wants and
then rebuilds the nest.*

*Through trial and error, the wrens always manage to get
even the long sticks through the small entrance hole.*

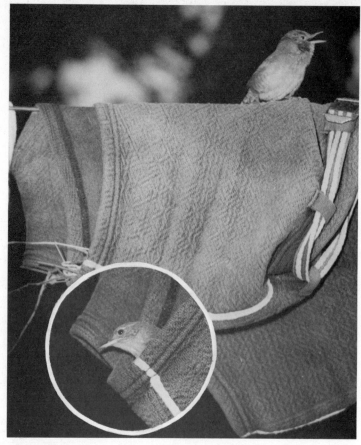

When it comes to wren nests, the uncommon is fairly common. One pair raised a family in a bathing suit left hanging on a clothesline.

Another clothesline garment wrens used as a nesting site was this pair of work pants.

Wrens are not particular about the kinds of houses in which they nest. This one found a coconut shell to its liking.

Conventional wren houses with 1¼-inch-diameter entrance holes are acceptable to wrens as long as they are placed in trees that provide cover.

Wrens do, of course, use standard wren houses without hesitation. Many people like to build their own, but they are easily obtained commercially, too. The most important thing to keep in mind is the size of the entrance hole. For wrens, it should be 1 to 1¼ inches. This is large enough to admit the tiny wrens, but will keep out starlings, house sparrows and predators. The opening may be round, or it may be 1 to 1¼ inches high and several inches wide—a possible help to the wrens when they attempt to bring in 4-inch-long twigs. Regardless of shape, through trial and error, they always manage to get the stick in anyway.

Historically, wrens nested in natural cavities, and they continue to do so today in more remote areas.

FUSSBUDGET FEMALE

Though we provide several wren houses in our yard, it seems the female always chooses the same funny house in the same century-old apple tree when she accompanies the male on their real estate tour. Typical of female wrens, she immediately sets about undoing her mate's well-intentioned work. Twig by twig, she throws out all the material that he brought in, at the same time clearly voicing her opinion of his nest-building talents. The two seem to get into terrible rows, scolding and fussing furiously. But the job gets done, and within two or three days, the nest is ready.

When complete, the nesting hole will be well filled. One wren nest, when it was taken apart for analysis, filled a two-gallon pail.

In their selection of building materials, house wrens are almost as eccentric as they are about the building site. One nest was made entirely of metal in the form of rusty bent nails, double-pointed tacks and pieces of wire. Another nest, found in Iowa, reportedly contained "52 hairpins, 68 nails (large), 120 small nails, 4 tacks, 13 staples, 10 pins, 4 pieces of pencil lead, 11 safety pins, 6 paper fasteners, 52 wires, 1 buckle, 2 hooks, 3 garter fasteners, and 2 odds and ends." These were probably the dummy nests of males, who tend to build them somewhat crudely. Just ask the females!

A more typical wren nest would have a foundation of twigs upon which the female has woven a liner of grass, rootlets, feathers, hair, wool, and, yes, she'll throw in a little rubbish, too—a scrap of Kleenex, a bit of yarn, for example.

While the female arranges the nest to her liking, the male stands guard and sometimes starts another nest which may be used later for a second brood. "He may also take up with a second female, for just as his mate is a shrew, he is a philanderer," wrote Alexander Wetmore. There is one report of eight active house wren nests on a property in Minnesota, but at no time were more than two males observed.

When the construction project is finished, the female lays an egg a day until there is a full clutch. Usually there are six to eight tiny white eggs thickly speckled with cinnamon-brown dots.

Only the female incubates the eggs, yet when the young hatch 13

Pugnaciously territorial, this male house wren is ready to do battle with his reflection.

days later, the male joins her in the feeding responsibilities.

The tireless parents have a strong instinct to provide an uninterrupted flow of food to their young from dawn to dusk. No nine-to-five hours for these diminutive parents! One male wren, whose mate had been killed, was counted making 1,217 trips in a single day with food for his little ones. Someone figured out that he was averaging a visit every 47 seconds, and that doesn't take into account the forays he made to feed himself.

Though I see it many times each summer, it still delights me to watch the male wren approach the nesting box with a billful of juicy caterpillar or some other squirming insect. He manages to sing all the way into the house without dropping any of the food. Whereas his song was a territorial advertisement a few weeks before, and then an outpouring of desire for the female, it now serves as a feeding stimulus to the youngsters in the nest. When we are nearby, we can hear the chicks inside the box peep an excited response to his song. The female's approach to the nest is quieter and more secretive, with several stops along a zigzag route before she actually enters the box. But she, too, lets the chicks know that food's on the way, with a raspy little rattling call. They respond just as excitedly to that as they do to the male's song.

Newly hatched baby wrens—like most very young birds—have an appearance that only a mother could love. Their covering is scant, with usually no more than 25 sepia-brown down feathers. And, like the other birds in this book, they are deaf at this stage and their eyes are sealed. But they have very large stomachs, larger than those of their parents. As they mature, their stomachs gradually shrink.

Tests have shown that food passes completely through the nestlings in about an hour and a half, so the supply must be continually replenished. Their stomachs are seldom empty, because their parents have an overwhelming urge to feed.

In fact, it's not uncommon for a wren that has been unsuccessful in finding a mate, or for some other reason has failed to nest, to feed other baby birds. Here's one account:

"The female grosbeak was on the nest and a house wren was bringing small caterpillars to her, which she took from the wren's beak and fed to her young," reported V. G. Hills. "At first it seemed to me as though the wren was liable to be cited as co-respondent, but soon the male grosbeak came and relieved his mate

Usually house wrens lay six to eight tiny white eggs thickly speckled with cinnamon-brown dots.

Only the female wren incubates the eggs, a 13-day task.

The male wren approaches the nest with a billful of squirming insects, managing to sing all the way into the house without dropping any of the food.

on the nest. Yet the wren continued to come with food which the male grosbeak likewise received and fed to the young. Both of the grosbeaks sometimes themselves ate the wren's offerings, in place of feeding them to their young. The wren made more trips to the nest than both grosbeaks combined." Hill said that after the grosbeak youngsters fledged, the wren fed them directly, and a few days later was observed feeding a family of house sparrows, natural enemies of wrens!

CREEPY-CRAWLY RIGHTS CAN PROMPT GENOCIDE

From the day it hatches to the end of its life, the wren's diet is 98 percent insects. About half of that is grasshoppers and beetles, the rest spiders, caterpillars and other insects. It is imperative, then, that a sufficient quantity of insects is available in the immediate vicinity of the nest at all times. To share this food supply with another wren family, or any other bird family, might prove disastrous for both. This is probably why the wren has evolved a practice which has earned it the reputation of "scoundrel" among some birders. In establishing and defending his territory, the male house wren may destroy the nest, eggs or young—even adult birds—of wrens or other songbirds on or near his home ground. This seems to occur in years when the population density of wrens is high.

Hal Harrison told us about a towhee nest with four eggs that was built on the ground within 40 feet of an occupied wren box. "One day, I saw the wren fly from the vicinity of the towhee nest," he said. "On examination, I found each of the four towhee eggs with a hole in it . . . the size of a wren's bill."

READY TO FACE THE WORLD

When the wren chicks leave the nest at the age of about two weeks, their down has worn away and they are clothed in their juvenile plumage, differing from their parents' only in the black mottling on their breast.

For a week or so after fledging, the wren chicks are still dependent on the adults for food. The family stays loosely together, and at dusk the parents round up their brood and settle into a roosting area for the night. They might use these roosts until the family disperses at the end of the week when the young have learned to hunt for their own food.

Wrens nest twice each summer, once in about the middle of May and again around late June. They do not pair permanently. Not only do they change mates from one year to the next, but about 60 percent switch partners between their first and second nestings. Often, one or both of the parents will begin a new nesting cycle before the first brood is independent. Yet, except under the most unusual circumstances, they energetically complete all their parental duties without missing a beat. Busy, busy, busy.

MAKING ITS WAY AGAINST SUPERIOR ODDS

Out in the world on its own, the young wren finds life fraught with peril. Some claim its number-one enemy is the cat. That's probably because wrens commonly nest close to humans, and humans often keep pets. Bird species that are shy of people don't seem to have such problems. We have two cats ourselves, but they are very content to spend their lives indoors, watching the birds through the window.

Wren mortality isn't entirely due to cats satisfying their instincts, however. Wrens are also preyed upon by foxes, snakes and red squirrels and by bird-eating raptors such as hawks, owls and shrikes.

Another primary enemy, because of competition for nesting sites, is the house sparrow. As bold, impudent and feisty as the wren may be, it can't drive out the sparrow. The house wren used to be a common bird in New England until the house sparrow was introduced in the late 1800s. However, since house sparrows thrive around horses, and since horses have pretty much disappeared from our daily lives, house sparrows are on the decline. As a result, the house wren is making a comeback in the areas of the Northeast where it nearly disappeared during the house sparrow's heyday.

One wren was seen making 1,217 trips in a single day with food for its offspring.

HOUSE WREN OR WOOD WREN?

By late August, the new wrens of the year have lost the black mottling on their breast and have acquired their first winter plumage. They are now virtually indistinguishable from the older birds, whose complete adult summer plumage is made up of about 1,200 contour feathers.

This late-summer plumage is duller and grayer than the spring courtship garb. In addition to the difference in their fall attire, the wrens undergo a personality change, too. No longer their usual belligerent, inquisitive selves, they become quiet recluses, deserting backyard gardens in favor of the deep woods where they retreat to the underbrush. Audubon actually thought he was observing a different and distinct species when he saw the house wren at this time of year, and he called it the "wood wren."

The house wren's song might still be heard in late July, but it diminishes in August. By late September or early October, most house wrens have left their summer homes and are back on their

It is not uncommon for a wren that has had an unsuccessful nesting to feed the young of other birds, such as this baby chimney swift.

wintering grounds in the Deep South. Typical of their winter personality, they travel alone, or perhaps in twos, but never in flocks. They are usually solitary until the breeding urge stirs in them again the following spring.

Then, the old birds will return to the place they nested the previous year. One study showed that there was a 75 percent return ratio of adults to the same or other nesting boxes on the premises. The one-year-olds, returning to breed for the first time, will try for a territory close to where they were hatched, but if it is occupied, they will disperse to more distant areas.

EASY TO LURE TO YOUR GARDEN

For all their compatibility with humans, house wrens are not in the habit of dining at feeding stations. Content with their insect diet, they are not tempted by the usual seed and suet offerings at feeders. However, if wrens are common in your area, they are easy to attract to your premises if you provide proper nesting houses for them. As mentioned earlier, either homemade or commercial houses, of almost any design, will be fine. The most important consideration is the size of the opening. It should be 1¼ inches in diameter, or 1¼ inches high by 3 or 4 inches long. This will permit easy access for the dainty wrens, but will keep out competitive house sparrows and starlings as well as predators. Consider a hanging house that can swing in the breeze. The wrens don't mind the motion, but it seems to effectively discourage house sparrows and predators.

A FAVORITE AROUND THE WORLD

There are over 50 species of wrens in the world, nine of which occur in North America. Our house wren is sometimes called the jenny wren, a nickname given the bird by early English settlers in America who were reminded of the little wren of their homeland. Surprisingly, the European "jenny" wren is the same species as our winter wren, *Troglodytes troglodytes*.

During migration periods or in winter months, the winter wren is sometimes seen poking about the underbrush. It is our smallest wren, even tinier than the house wren, with a much shorter, stubby, upturned tail. On its New England and Canadian breeding grounds or in winter quarters from Ohio south to Texas and Florida, this midget bird prefers to stay close to the ground.

One of the house wren's cousins is the Carolina wren, the largest of the eastern wrens.

The giant of North American wrens, the cactus wren is well named. It lives and builds its nest in a fortress of cactus spines.

In the eastern United States, the Carolina wren is common in thick underbrush in the Southeast. It is found as far north as Massachusetts (a few each year), Rhode Island and Connecticut, except when there are severe winters which either wipe it out or force it southward. It is the largest of the eastern wrens, and differs in appearance from the house wren in that it has a broad white eye stripe and is generally brighter-colored—more rufous on its back, buffy underneath. And, unlike the house wren, it is a regular visitor to backyard bird feeders, where it enjoys the suet offered. The easiest way to identify it, however, is by its song, a persistent *tea-ket-tle, tea-ket-tle, tea-ket-tle, tea-ket-tle.*

Like its close relative the house wren, the Carolina takes to nesting boxes and shares some of its cousin's penchant for unusual site selection. A woman in Captiva, Florida, discovered one day that her clothes dryer was overheating. When she checked the opening to the vent on the outside of her house, she discovered a Carolina wren incubating a clutch of eggs in a bulky nest in the vent pipe.

In wetland areas, the marsh wren *(Cistothorus palustris)* or the sedge wren *(Cistothorus platensis)* might be heard.

In the West, the common wrens, in addition to the house wren, are the rock, Bewick's, canyon and cactus wrens, the last of which is the giant of North American wrens. In fact, I think the cactus wren is quite un-wrenlike compared to the other wrens. It often measures nearly nine inches in length, seldom cocks its long tail, and likes to build its bulb-shaped nest in cholla cactus.

K. P. H.

HOUSE WREN FACTS

Description: A tiny, jaunty bird, less than half the size of a robin. Drab brown in plumage but perky in personality, with an uptilted tail that reflects the bird's moods.

Habitat: Underbrush and thickets, woodlands, gardens, orchards.

Nest and Eggs: Often nests in birdhouses. Otherwise, in almost any cavity or niche that it can get into—clothes left hanging on the line, watering pots, and fishing creels are some of the places that have been used. May be from 5–8 eggs, commonly 6 or 7. White with heavy cinnamon-colored speckles, sometimes giving the entire egg a pinkish cast.

Food: Almost 100 percent insects.

Life Span: If it survives the first year, it will probably live 2 or 3 years. One wren was known to live to the age of 7 years, 2 months in the wild.

Song: Its most distinctive characteristic: a rollicking, bubbling, energetic tumble of notes that's hard to describe.

Cunning, inquisitive, an admirable mimic and full of mischief, the blue jay is "king of the hill" at the feeding station.

CHAPTER NINE

Blue Jay—A Mixed Bag of Tricks

Panic!

A feeding station loaded with goldfinches, purple finches, juncos, tree sparrows and a downy woodpecker suddenly erupts in bedlam as the shriek of a hawk is heard.

Feathers fly. Every bird is airborne and streaking for the nearest cover. Where dozens of songbirds fed a few seconds earlier, not a bird is seen.

Then the hawk appears. Wait . . . it isn't a hawk after all. It's a blue jay imitating the call of a hawk. A cocky jay, dressed in flashy blue-and-white feathers, sails onto one of the feeders and begins to eat wherever and whatever he likes—for the blue jay is king of the hill, cock of the feeders.

It is this kind of loud, show-off, "bully" behavior that has earned for the blue jay the fear of most songbirds and the disdain of some people. Perhaps the blue jay's behavior reminds them of people they dislike.

Chasing other birds away from the feeding station, however, may be one of the least of the jay's offenses. Some allege that it raids nests, eats eggs and sometimes even eats young birds.

"The trouble with the blue jay is that we all fall in love with him in the winter when he is being good, but lose sight of him in the spring and summer when he is practicing his villainies," wrote ornithologist W. L. Dawson. Apparently Dawson, like us, enjoyed having blue jays at his winter feeding station. Many people do not.

"Whatever you do, don't photograph blue jays on our feeders," was the request of a prominent bird-feeder manufacturer. "People just don't like blue jays and if they see them using feeders, they may not buy the products," he claimed.

Well, what about these charges against the blue jay? Aggressive? Yes. Intelligent? Very. Mischievous? Without a doubt. But a bird to be hated? I seriously doubt the blue jay deserves that kind of bum rap. It is simply behaving like a typical member of the family Corvidae, which includes 16 North American species of crows, ravens, magpies and other jays. Indeed, the intelligence of all the corvids is to be respected.

The blue jay is a forest bird that also thrives in backyard shade trees of cities, towns and villages.

The blue jay's loud, show-off, bully personality has earned for it the fear of songbirds and the disdain of some people.

When I was a boy helping my dad photograph birds, we often had blue jays and crows living in our home. Keeping wild birds as pets is illegal now, but it wasn't in those days. I'm glad I had the experience of keeping jays and crows, because I learned firsthand how intelligent they are. I remember that it was not safe to leave anything shiny lying around the house when the birds were loose. Invariably, they would pick up these objects and carry them around or stash them where I couldn't find them. They even learned our lifestyle well enough to know when it was feeding time by watching us remove certain food containers from the refrigerator.

"Cunning, inquisitive, an admirable mimic, full of mischief; in some localities extremely shy, in others exactly the reverse, it is difficult to paint him in his true colors," claimed Charles Bendire, a 19th-century ornithologist. Maybe Bendire's statement explains why some of us love having the blue jays in our backyards, while others don't. In New England, for example, where blue jays seem to be most disliked, they are abundant and are often considered pest birds at feeding stations. In the Midwest, where there are fewer blue jays, they are a delight to have around. Perhaps numbers make the real difference.

NO SHRINKING VIOLET

Everyone agrees that blue jays are noisy and boisterous, giving the impression that they are independent, lawless, haughty and even impudent. Washington Irving referred to the bird as "that noisy coxcomb, in his gay light blue coat and white underclothing."

Certainly one of the bird's most outstanding characteristics is its noisiness. A bird of many voices, most of them loud, *Cyanocitta cristata* gets its genus name from the Greek *kyanos* (blue), and *kitta* (chattering bird).

Its best-known noise is its "jay" call. Shrieked in a demanding tone, *jay, jay, jay* is given when the bird discovers danger or an owl

Courtship is a very private affair for blue jays, involving bobbing up and down and chasing about in a quiet manner, sometimes even at feeders.

to be tormented. Henry David Thoreau commented on the "unrelenting steel-cold scream of a jay, unmelted, that never flows into a song. A sort of wintry trumpet, screaming cold, hard, tense, frozen music, like the winter sky itself."

A far more musical form of that call is a quieter two-noted version, a bell-like *tull-ull,* which the jay utters while raising and lowering its head. Females will utter the rapid clicking call that sounds like *tea-cup*.

Then there is the so-called whisper call. A surprise coming from a bird with so many loud noises, the whisper call is a soft, musical vocalization employed by the male during courtship to reassure the female that his attentions are nonaggressive. Some think the whisper call sounds like the song of the catbird.

BEAUTY IN THE AZURE CLAN

Everyone also concedes that blue jays are strikingly beautiful birds. At 11–12½ inches, they are slightly larger than robins. Their upperparts, crest, nape, back and tail are bright blue, decorated with a prominent black necklace bordering a white face and throat. Their underparts are light gray or white. They have bold white spots in their wings and on the outer edges of their tails. Eyes are dark. Sexes are identical.

Blue jays also have a very distinct flight. I watched one fly across a Wisconsin sunset not long ago, and though I saw only a silhouette, I knew immediately what it was. Its steady yet rather slow wingbeat is like no other. I recognized its characteristically strong, level flight, direct and unwavering. Its crest and bill were very obvious. Seen in bright daylight, the azure garb adds striking beauty to any landscape.

Found almost everywhere east of the Rocky Mountains, the blue jay is the only jay throughout most of its range. Once considered a shy bird of the remote woodlands, today the blue jay thrives in backyard shade trees of cities, suburbs and villages. It has adapted well to man's imposition on the land and is as much at home in a private garden as a public park. It is a forest bird that can be found on the woodlots of most farms east of the Rockies.

A MERRY OLD TIME OF COURTING

Winter bands of blue jays break up in the early spring as the courting season starts. Depending on geographic location, blue jays begin courting from February to May.

In the jay family, however, courtship is not a very private affair. It usually involves one female and several males. Ornithologist Arthur Cleveland Bent described what he thought was a courting scene. He "saw a flock of seven or eight blue jays having a merry time in the top of a large oak in my backyard. They were apparently courting. I could not distinguish the sexes, of course. Perhaps there was only one female, and the males were all following her. . . . Several of them, presumably males, were bobbing up and down. They were constantly changing places in the tree and chasing each other about. At least one was evidently trying to escape, or perhaps starting a game of 'follow the leader.' Finally, one did fly away and all the others trooped after it."

After mating, the blue jay pair will become very quiet and secretive, a most un-jaylike behavior. First, the pair will collect twigs and carry them around until they find a suitable nesting site. This stick-carrying behavior is so well known that people in the South humorously claim that "the jaybird carries sticks to the devil."

Some blue jays will select nesting sites right in the main traffic patterns of people, like this one in Wildwood, Pennsylvania.

The well-hidden nest, built by both adults, is usually 10–25 feet above the ground in the crotch of a tree.

WELL-HIDDEN NESTS

Those sticks eventually wind up in a well-hidden, bulky nest, usually in the crotch or outer branches of a coniferous or deciduous tree, 10–25 feet above the ground. Both sexes build the nest, using thorny twigs, bark, mosses, string, leaves and a lining of rootlets.

It is not unusual for blue jays to appropriate the nest of another bird. In Peoria, Illinois, blue jays stole the nest of a pair of robins, fixed it up to suit themselves and laid their eggs in it, "before the eyes of the angry robins."

Blue jays normally lay a clutch of four or five eggs in their bulky nest of twigs, bark, mosses and rootlets.

Blue jay parents share the 17–18-day incubation.

Apparently there are both shy and gregarious blue jays. Though all are very secretive, some will nest away from human habitation, in coniferous forests, crab apple thickets and other remote spots. Others, strangely, will select sites right in the main traffic patterns of people. My father was surprised to learn that a blue jay nested in a rose trellis attached to the front porch of a Wildwood, Pennsylvania, home. Members of the family daily used the porch and walked within a foot or two of the nest without disturbing the incubating or brooding bird. In Massachusetts, blue jays built a nest on a crossbeam of an electric-light pole that stood near a flight of steps used all day long by people coming and going to a train station. The nest was so close to the people that one man claimed he could touch the incubating jay with his umbrella. Another jay nested in a begonia pot on a porch railing in Amherst, Massachusetts.

Normally, blue jays will lay a clutch of four or five eggs. They are uniformly oval, olive or buff-colored with dark brown or grayish spots. Both birds incubate, though the female probably does most of the stint through the 17–18 days required for the eggs to hatch. One woman who watched the nesting cycle of a blue jay family at close range reported that the male aided in building the nest and that both birds incubated, "each relieving the other at more or less regular intervals." And "the bird at play did not forget its imprisoned mate, but returned now and then with a choice bit of food, which was delivered with various little demonstrations of sympathy and affection."

There is another interesting little behavior trait that the male blue jay seems to follow as he approaches the nest. Instead of flying directly to the nest, he will fly to the base of the tree in which the nest is located. He will then hop silently, circling his way up the tree on what some call the invisible "spiral staircase." He will use this subterfuge to deliver food to his mate who is either incubating or brooding young.

BEWARE OF PROTECTIVE PARENTS

Blue jays can be downright dangerous to humans or other predators who come too close to their nests. Some pairs attack intruders with such fierceness that they have been known to draw blood.

The youngsters learn to make noise at an early age. They are quite good at screaming even before they leave the nest.

Dad and I have found out while photographing blue jays at their nests that they are rather easy subjects if the photographer is willing to withstand the attacks and terrific scoldings that one must undergo while setting up equipment. Blue jays will usually treat prowling cats, dogs, squirrels and other potential predators in a similar manner.

On the other hand, ornithologist Donald J. Nicholas had to lift an incubating blue jay off its nest to examine the eggs. He then placed the motionless bird back on the nest and left. Dad has had that same experience with the blue jay's cousin, the scrub jay, in Florida.

At 17 days, the young blue jays are nearly ready to leave the nest.

Fledgling blue jays are cute beyond description with their new blue-and-white feathers and stubby tails.

HATCHLINGS ARE HELPLESS

When the young hatch, they are limp, blind and naked. Like most other songbirds at that age, about the only movement of which they are capable is holding their head up for their first feeding. According to John Ronald Arnold, who studied the blue jay for his doctorate, nesting blue jays open their eyes on the fifth day. At that age, they also have enough strength in their legs to grasp the lining of the nest with their claws. "During the eighth and ninth days the feathers in all the body tracts except the head and neck regions begin to break from their sheaths," Arnold reports. By day 17, the nestlings resemble adult blue jays, and they are ready to fledge at 17–21 days.

Fledgling blue jays are cute beyond description, with their new blue-and-white feathers and stubby tails. While I was helping my dad photograph a family of baby blue jays that had just left the nest at Cook Forest State Park, Pennsylvania, one baby flew under our log cabin. This predicament produced an unforgettable day. We couldn't crawl under the cabin to reach the bird, nor would it come

out regardless of what we did to coax it. Frankly, I can't recall how we did get it out, but out it did come after hours of effort. I do remember what a great relief it was to return the jay to its noisy, scolding parents.

The youngsters, too, learn to make noise at an early age. In fact, they are quite good at screaming even before they leave the nest.

In northern areas, like Cook Forest, blue jays usually have only one brood a year. Farther south they have two, occasionally three.

Parental care is unusually long. There are reports of blue jays being fed until they were four months old. Nevertheless, fledgling jays grow rapidly, and in three weeks to a month, they are difficult to distinguish from adults. They experience their first plumage molt 50–90 days after they leave the nest. Adults also molt during this period and grow a very similar winter garb.

I have to laugh every time I think of how weird our blue jays look when they are in their late-summer molt. For some reason, they lose all of the feathers around their neck and head at the same time. They look hideous. We call them "Frankensteins."

THEY WILL EAT ANYTHING

Like their close relatives the crows, ravens and magpies, jays will eat almost anything; they are omnivorous. Much of this is due to their fabulous bills, which are adept at opening almost anything. "Stout, sharp-pointed, almost as tough as steel, they can be used to hammer, crush, crack, probe, split and tear," Olin Sewall Pettingill, Jr., said about corvid bills. "If man could invent a tool as simple and powerful, he would make a fortune. No nut is too hard for a corvid to crack."

Some 75 percent of what blue jays eat is vegetable matter, with nuts and seeds being high on their preferred list. They are especially fond of acorns, beechnuts and corn. For that reason, they spend a great deal of their time cruising oak and beech woods, plucking acorns as they go. A jay may carry one acorn in its bill and one in its throat, as it heads for a suitable place to bury them. Many wild-life biologists credit both the blue jay and the gray squirrel with the reforestation of the hardwoods of North America. The same was true for the American chestnut before the devastating blight.

Other vegetable matter that blue jays regularly eat include apples, strawberries, currants, chokecherries, wild grapes, serviceberries, elderberries, hawthorns, pokeberries and the seeds of sumac, sorrel and other grains. In Florida, the blue jay thrives on palmetto seeds.

Animal matter that blue jays eat includes such interesting items as beetles, grasshoppers and caterpillars. They also savor snails, small fish, frogs, salamanders, mice and possibly some small birds as well as some birds' eggs and young.

Those great bills are also used as handles for tools. In his book *Ravens, Crows, Magpies and Jays* Tony Angell describes a jay's use of tools: "Captive blue jays were able to retrieve food from outside their cage by actually manufacturing and using a tool. Restricted by an enclosure that would not permit them to reach food pellets with their bill alone, the birds tore out strips of newspaper and used them as 'rakes' to reach out and pull back the food to the point where it could be retrieved and eaten." He told of another captive jay that raised the water level of its drinking dish by placing solid objects in the container. The water was thus raised to where the jay could reach it—à la Aesop's crow.

While these fledglings were being photographed, one flew under a log cabin and refused to come out for several hours.

ANTING—A STRANGE BEHAVIOR

Before leaving the subject of the blue jay's diet, some mention should be made of "anting." Though not related to eating, it does involve a food of birds: ants.

Anting begins when the bird flies to an anthill or a swarm of ants and allows the insects to crawl on it. This submissive behavior will permit either the ants to enter the bird's feathers or the bird to pick up the ants and insert them into its feathers. The strange effect the ants have on the bird is even more curious. The bird will begin preening or combing the feathers under its wings, along its tail and around its vent. The preening is often so vigorous and violent that the bird staggers or even somersaults due to a lack of balance.

Describing his many observations of anting among birds that he kept in a large aviary, H. Roy Ivor wrote, "The wings are spread and held spread to some extent during the performance and the greatest effort seems to be made to rub the ant on the underside of the tail. This effort, which should be so easy, is the cause of the

Parental care is unusually long. There are reports of blue jays being fed until they were four months old.

comical contortions always prominent. They try continually to bring the tail under them to such an extent that they often tumble on their back while so doing and many times I have actually seen them sitting on their tail. . . . It is a most comical sight which will nearly bring tears of laughter to the eyes."

The exact reasons for anting are still unknown, but the theories boil down to: (1) inducing sexual or other sensual pleasure; (2) utilizing the formic acid or some other substance contained in the ants to repel parasites; or (3) soothing, via ant substances, irritated skin. Since anting occurs most often during the late-summer molting period when new feathers are being grown, the skin-soothing suggestion is favored by many researchers over the sexual or antiparasitic theories.

Whatever the reasons, blue jays and many other backyard birds really get a kick out of anting.

JOIN THE MOB SCENE

By late August and early September, youngsters and oldsters join together in troops. These small flocks of several families spend their days cruising the mature forests searching for acorns and other fruits of the season. They keep in touch with soft conversational chatter as they range through the woodlands.

One of the better-known habits of these bands of jays is to pester owls and hawks. If a jay discovers a sleeping owl or a hawk hidden in foliage, it sends out a cry to which all jays within hearing respond. The screaming mob will then proceed to drive the owl out of hiding and force it to fly from tree to tree seeking refuge. Tony Angell says, "Along our creek, jays continuously utter invitations to 'come and mob.' These are the *wah* calls. Over the years I have learned to distinguish between the 'come mob an owl' and 'come mob a squirrel.' The owl-mobbing call is likely to be sustained for as long as it takes to drive the predator from the neighborhood, perhaps an hour or more."

These vocal communiqués also provide protection to other woodland inhabitants. Every creature in hearing range may be informed of the presence of a predator long before the predator is in sight. Deer hunters, for example, are not very pleased with blue jays that announce the hunters' presence to every deer in the area.

THE TABLES CAN TURN

Blue jays are not always on the giving end of a fight. They, too, suffer casualties from predators, particularly from hawks. The jay's defense against marauding broad-winged, red-shouldered, Cooper's and sharp-shinned hawks is to fly into the nearest woodland, dodging between leaves and branches with an agility that can't be matched by the hawk. Caught in the open, however, the blue jay is defenseless. Sometimes, however, blue jays will come to the aid of another of their kind in trouble. Angell tells about a sharp-shinned hawk pursuing a blue jay: "The hunter was leaping over branches and snatching at the tail of the breathless jay that was staying just out of reach. Then, quite suddenly, two other jays entered the stand, fresh, alert and scolding. They bounded about and above the hawk, who turned her attention toward them. The first jay used the distraction of the hawk to make an escape to the cover of another cluster of trees. The two other jays retreated slowly into the thickest of the sumac branches leaving the fatigued hawk behind." Angell suggests that the two jays were apparently exercising an act of altruism, for they were, by all appearances, risking their own survival to enhance the possible survival of another individual. Such behavior is not uncommon in the corvid family.

SOME MIGRATE; SOME DON'T

As winter approaches, the troops either settle into a region to spend the winter or start their long flights south. No one can explain why some blue jays migrate and others don't. Because they are a common bird of northern feeding stations, it would appear that a significant number of them must not migrate. However, a significant number do, as thousands are seen migrating each year from key observation spots across the East and upper Midwest.

Acorns and other wild nuts are among the blue jay's favorite foods.

Aside from wild nuts, blue jays are fond of sunflower seeds, beef suet and cracked corn at feeding stations.

While blue jays will use almost any kind of sunflower-seed feeder, they prefer one with a flat surface. They aren't as comfortable on small perches.

Blue jays seem to favor the same flyways as other migratory species. Such well-known lookouts as Hawk Mountain, Pennsylvania; Cape May, New Jersey; Point Pelee, Ontario; and the shorelines of the Great Lakes are all fine locations from which to see the flights of blue jays headed south in the fall and, to a lesser extent, north in the spring.

Maurice Broun, the first curator at Hawk Mountain Sanctuary, once counted 1,535 blue jays passing the lookout there on a single day in October.

Instead of migrating in a large flock like some birds, blue jays are more cautious. They invariably are grouped in very loose, strung-out flocks of 12–25 birds. When you see one, you usually see others following at some distance.

Water is important to blue jays and birdbaths will draw them into backyards.

Erie County, Pennsylvania, was the location of my most memorable blue jay flight. I was then editor of Pennsylvania *Game News* magazine and was interested in doing a story about this phenomenon. I met a game protector in the northwest corner of the state who drove me to the shore of Lake Erie to see the September spectacle. It was worth seeing. Though I don't remember how many blue jays we actually watched pass over, it had to be in the many hundreds. Like other corvids, the blue jays were not protected in Pennsylvania at that time. Therefore, the shooting of these tempting targets along the Lake Erie shore was not illegal in the early 1960s. My game protector friend and I witnessed a shooting gallery that was reminiscent of the days when hawk slaughters were legal along those same flyways. Like the hawk's, the blue jay's tarnished reputation was all that was needed for even conservation-minded gunners to feel sanctimonious.

My feelings about the blue jay were summed up by Tony Angell when he said of corvids: "To some they are the apotheosis of avian form and a spirit worthy of the highest artistic tribute. Others consider them as competitors, more to be destroyed than admired. It's hard to imagine that anyone professing sensitivity would not recognize these birds as a most remarkable consolidation of highly evolved animal social systems, physical apparatus, skills and beauty."

BLUE JAYS LIKE BACKYARD THICKETS

Blue jays are easy to attract to the backyard feeding station. However, the three basic needs of all birds—food, water and cover—are necessary to maintain a resident population of blue jays.

The kind of cover blue jays require for both feeding and nesting is an abundance of small, thick trees and shrubs. These include crab apple, any of the evergreens, oaks, hickory, beech, hawthorns, sumac, wild grape and many others. Cover is perhaps the most important basic need that birds require before they will feel comfortable in any backyard.

Aside from the natural nuts, seeds and fruits produced by a well-planted backyard, blue jays might be attracted to feeding stations that offer beef suet, sunflower seeds and cracked corn.

Every species has its own way of eating. The seed eaters, in particular, have their own special way of cracking or consuming the various kinds of feeding-station fare. The blue jay is no exception. It reminds me of a chipmunk as it fills its gullet and then its mouth with as many seeds as it can carry. Later, the jay will regurgitate them and either bury or consume them in private.

Jays will use almost any kind of bird feeder, but like cardinals, they prefer to have a flat surface to stand on. Perches are too precarious, and therefore, a tray feeder or a seed tray mounted under a cylinder bird feeder will better suit them.

Water is important and will draw blue jays into a backyard, particularly if the water is moving or splashing. Dripping or flowing water has a magnetic attraction to almost all species of songbirds. If that kind of water area is not possible in your yard, then the standard ceramic birdbath is much better than no water at all. Blue jays bathe and drink at our three-tiered, recycling water area on our patio through much of the year, though the energy crunch has kept us from heating our water area during recent winters.

Planting and planning a backyard to attract nesting blue jays is a much greater problem. Blue jays are very independent creatures and despite the fact that you may have provided all the required nesting cover, they are apt to choose a site somewhere away from your eyes. Though there are records of blue jays nesting in porch trellises, they are more apt to select a secretive thicket in which to raise their broods.

THE OTHER JAYS

The blue jay has seven North American cousin jays, many of them visitors to the backyards of the regions in which they live. All but two live entirely in the West.

The two exceptions also live in the extreme north and south. The gray jay or Canada jay, *Perisoreus canadensis,* is common in the

The scrub jay is a crestless jay that visits backyards in Florida and most of the West.

cool northern coniferous forests, especially around lumber camps across much of Canada and Alaska. It occurs in the northern areas of the upper Midwest and New England, but in the West it ranges south all the way to Baja. It is a large, fluffy, gray bird, larger than a robin, with a black patch or partial cap across the back of its head and a white forehead.

The other is the scrub jay, *Aphelocoma coerulescens,* a crestless jay living in Florida and in most of the West. A lovely blue-colored jay, it is often found living in the same Florida yards as the blue jay. The scrub jay lacks the crest and the white wing and tail patches found in the blue jay. In Florida, the scrub jay feeds on palmetto seeds and is so tame that it will eat from people's hands. In the West, it thrives on the scrub oak for which it was probably named.

The most common backyard "blue jay" in the West, and the only crested jay found there, is Steller's, *Cyanocitta stelleri.* This large, dark-headed jay with no white is a frequent visitor to backyards located in or near coniferous forests or mixed pine and oak woodlands. Hybrids between Steller's and blue jays have been discovered in Colorado.

Three other western jays—green, gray-breasted and brown—are found only in the Southwest and along the Mexican border, and are unlikely backyard visitors.

The pinyon jay ranges widely in the Rocky Mountain region and in the Sierras and Cascades of the Far West.

G. H. H.

BLUE JAY FACTS

Description: A noisy blue bird with a crest, white spots in wings and tail; whitish or light gray underparts; black necklace and black eyes; slightly larger than a robin.

Habitat: Eastern forests, farms, parks, cities, villages and suburban backyards. Extending its western range.

Nest and Eggs: Bulky, well-hidden nest in crotch or on branch of coniferous or deciduous tree, 10–15 feet above the ground. The 4 or 5 eggs are olive or buff-colored with dark brown spots.

Food: About 75 percent vegetable matter, particularly acorns, beech nuts and corn; 25 percent insects, including caterpillars, beetles and grasshoppers. May eat an occasional bird's egg or young.

Life Span: If it survives its first year, a blue jay will probably live an average of about 5 years in the wild. One blue jay, banded on Long Island, was recaptured 13 years later in Laurel, Maryland. Another lived 15 years in the wild.

Song: Noisy bird with a number of call notes, ranging from its best-known *jay, jay, jay* to a bell-like *tull-ull* to a clicking call, *tea-cup.* The male's courtship song is a quiet whisper that resembles the quiet, disjointed song of a catbird.

The white-breasted nuthatch goes through life hitching down tree trunks headfirst.

CHAPTER TEN

White-breasted Nuthatch— The Upside-down Bird

It's easy to recognize the upside-down bird. It's the little bluish-gray imp that goes through life more upside down than right-side up, constantly hopping down tree trunks headfirst. Its real name is nuthatch, and it's on nearly everyone's list of best-loved backyard birds. Other tree-climbing birds don't even attempt such a feat.

Our European ancestors watched the topsy-turvy Old World nuthatches wedge nuts into crevices in bark and whack them open with their strong bills. The English named the birds "nuthack"; the French, "notehache."

The white-breasted nuthatch, *Sitta carolinensis,* is the largest of the North American nuthatches, a sedate, businesslike bird with a characteristic nasal call of *yank, yank, yank.* With a bit more tail, it would be about the size of a sparrow. As it is, the ¾-ounce bird measures less than six inches from the tip of its bill to the end of its short, square tail. Pearly blue-gray above, white below, it has a shiny black cap, beady black eyes, broad shoulders, short legs and a chestnut wash under its tail. The sexes are alike, but the black on the male's head is a deeper, truer black than the duller black on the female's.

Mixed woodlands, orchards, woodlots and backyards with shade trees are home to white-breasteds.

The white-breasted spends its life in the shade trees of forests, orchards, town and country woodlots and backyards from southern Canada to southern Mexico, with the exception of the treeless areas of the Great Plains and the desert.

NUTHATCH SPRING BEGINS IN JANUARY

Nuthatches are classified as songbirds, but their voices can hardly be regarded as musical. Their *yank-yank* calls are very nasal and sound like toots on a little toy horn.

Sometimes as early as January, we hear our resident male white-breasted begin his spring courtship song. He and his mate have stayed loosely together through the winter, often visiting our suet and sunflower seed feeders. Feeding in the same territory during the day, they retire to separate roosting holes at night. In the morning, the male leaves his roost, and within half an hour has established himself on a convenient perch and begun his "serenade." Generally, he starts before the light of day breaks through, and here in the North, often in subfreezing temperatures.

AN ENERGETIC COURTSHIP

Little was known about the actual courtship ritual of the nuthatch until Lawrence Kilham, a researcher working primarily in Lyme, New Hampshire, closely observed nuthatch behavior in the wild and in captivity between 1963 and 1970. His in-depth study has given us an intimate look at the sometimes bizarre love life of this little "tree mouse." His anecdotes are amusing as well as informative.

For example, he tells of one male who had recently acquired a mate. Within minutes of leaving his roost hole, the bird would fly to the topmost branch of one of the tallest oaks or maples. "He sang flat-sounding *what-whats* in a rapid series lasting two seconds," reported Kilham. Then the nuthatch rested for three seconds while slowly swaying his body in a 45-degree arc. "His head and neck would then suddenly shoot up so that his body was almost vertical as he began again," Kilham says. "A sudden change, often noted after five to ten minutes, was a shift from the dull *what* notes to musical *wurp, wurp, wurps*. On nearly all such occasions," Kilham continues, "I soon heard the first *kun* notes of the female. She was usually at a distance and in no hurry to arrive."

Other times, a female might join her singing mate on a perch below his. "After swaying slowly from side to side for a time, she then became motionless, as if held by his song," Kilham noted. Her mesmerization began when the male stretched to a vertical position and began bowing with each *wurp* he sang. With his back to her, he gave her a look at all his colors, showing them off to their best advantage as he bowed. First she saw his gleaming black crown and nape, then his blue-gray back, the black-and-white pattern of his spread tail, and finally, as he finished his deep bow, a flash of his chestnut flanks. Ecstasy! "The complete attention that a female can give to such a performance over a period of six to eight minutes is extraordinary!'' Kilham says. Nevertheless, after a while, the female will grow restless and fly off to begin feeding.

As a result of his years of observation, Kilham believes that intense displays such as these are generally performed by males who have recently acquired mates. After a pair bond is well established, the male's performance is less fervent. The pair might then sit side by side, touching, and rub their bills and necks together.

The male courts the female with a great deal of ritual. Often, he has his back to her to best show off all his colors.

The female usually watches him with undivided attention.

MALES LEARN TO BE GOOD FATHERS

These displays may continue through March. In addition, courtship feeding begins, a ritual that the pair practices throughout the nesting cycle.

The male hastens to his mate with a tasty morsel, but is likely to find her motionless, crouched low with bill pointed upward. The female will hold her position until the male aligns his bill with hers in just the right way. Only then will she accept his offering. Other times, her mate might bring her tempting, juicy caterpillars or small worms which she'll eat with gusto. Then, all of a sudden, she might refuse to take them. The male finally catches on to what she wants. He takes his offering and bashes it to a pulp, then tries again. This time she takes it, provided the male has his bill in just the right position.

Kilham says that one interpretation of why the female is so fussy is that she is "teaching" her mate, or more precisely, awakening his latent parental instincts, by playing the role of a nestling so young that it can manage only prey that is well-prepared ahead of time and placed directly into the baby's throat.

Later in the season, she'll crouch and quiver her wings, bill gaping, giving a *chrr* call like an older nestling.

FLOAT FOR JOY

Various forms of courtship feeding are fairly common among birds, and many species perform some type of elaborate courtship display to their mates. But the nuthatches have other traditions as well when it comes to wooing.

Sometimes, they suddenly start chasing each other madly for 20 seconds or so, zipping around and between tree trunks. Then, they settle down to their usual feeding as though nothing happened. Ten minutes later, they might start the whole wild chase all over again.

Other times, one or the other will suddenly launch off into a floating flight with wings stretched into a V. "The occasion appears to be sheer exuberance," Kilham tells us. He has seen a male float down to his mate just before instigating one of their frantic chases. Another male floated the last several feet to his nest hole when feeding his mate while she was sitting on eggs, and a female came to her nest hole in long floating flights as she carried in nesting material.

BIG TERRITORY FOR A LITTLE BIRD

The nesting territory is established around the middle of February. Each pair will have an area that encompasses 25–30 acres in a wooded region, and up to 50 acres if the vicinity is semiwooded. It may or may not be the same territory that served them during the winter as their foraging grounds.

If they are an established pair, they will most likely use the same nest site they used in previous years. Generally, this is a natural cavity 15–50 feet above the ground in a large, old shade tree. Sometimes they'll use a vacant woodpecker hole, and occasionally they can be enticed to a birdhouse, especially if it is covered with bark.

These are the same kinds of dens that squirrels, both red and gray, use for roosting and for raising their young, and competition for such homes is keen.

Typically, the nest is in a natural cavity 15–50 feet above the ground in a large shade tree.

Occasionally, they will use a birdhouse if it is placed in a location that appeals to them.

When the pair finds a vacant site that is acceptable to both, the construction project begins. The female builds the nest, though the male may assist by collecting some of the materials for her. Shreds of bark are carried in, often in lengths greater than the birds themselves. The bark is piled in the bottom of the nest cavity to a depth of about a half inch. Then the nest proper is built. More bark, but this time softer, inner pieces, is collected along with grasses, twigs, roots, and perhaps some fur, hair, or feathers. The female weaves these into a soft, feltlike mat upon which she will lay her eggs. Squirrel hair is often collected, and, if they can get it, rabbit hair.

One pair of nuthatches thought they had a real treasure when they found a bountiful source of easy-to-get rabbit fur. They discovered a dead rabbit—one that had been dead for some time, actually. The female wove the fur into their nest mat, and plunked the bunny's cottontail right in the center. The woman who found this nest said it smelled more like a buzzard's domicile than a nuthatch's home.

Nuthatches produce large sets of eggs—from five to nine. They raise only one brood a year.

*Though baby nuthatches cannot fly very well when they leave the nest,
they are top-notch climbers.*

ONE FAMILY A YEAR

The female lays one egg a day until the clutch is complete. Because nuthatches raise only one brood a year, they produce large
sets of eggs. There may be from five to nine eggs, but usually there
are eight. They are white, oval and prettily marked with heavy
brown or lavender spots.

During the egg-laying period, and throughout the female's 12-day
incubation, the male continues to bring food to his mate. In fact, the
female seems lethargic at this time, preferring to remain quiet and
close to her nest rather than forage for herself. At the beginning of
the season, this courtship feeding was a kind of refresher course in

The white-breasted en-joys hanging sunflower-seed feeders, taking one seed at a time.

The nuthatch flies to a nearby tree, wedges the seed into a crevice, and cracks it open.

parenthood, but now it serves another useful purpose. With the male providing a plentiful supply of insects for himself and for his mate, the female nuthatch is able to devote all her energy to laying and incubating the eggs. Later, when the eggs hatch and there are gaping mouths to feed, both adults will share the responsibility.

SWEEPING WITHOUT A BROOM

One of the curious rituals nuthatches perform during their nesting cycle is their habit of "sweeping" the area in and around their nesting cavity. Back and forth they sweep, using a motion similar to the one used by birds to wipe clean their bills after eating, except that they swing the whole body into an arc.

No one is really sure why nuthatches go through this routine, but there are a couple of theories. The most logical is that it is a territorial defense against their arch-rivals, the squirrels. They often hold insects in their bills as they sweep, and it's likely that some chemical in the crushed insects may repel squirrels.

Lawrence Kilham has surely seen more "bill-sweeping" than any of the rest of us. He says that both sexes sweep, sometimes working themselves into a real frenzy, sweeping hard for as long as 15 minutes nonstop. Often, the bill-sweeping begins immediately after the nuthatch spots a squirrel or chipmunk.

Usually, when the urge to sweep comes upon them, nuthatches grab a piece of insect from within inches of where they are and start right in. They have a habit of stashing things in the bark crevices around their nesting holes in the same way a dog buries a bone or a squirrel buries acorns. Into these niches go bits of insects, nuts, and some type of whitish feltlike material. If an insect isn't available, they'll sweep with just their bills.

If the sweeping fails to repel the squirrel, the nuthatch has another trick to protect its nest and young—the distraction display. Holding itself with wings and tail stiffly spread, bill pointing up, the nuthatch sways s-l-o-w-l-y from one side to the other, taking 10–20 seconds for each sway. The bird seems to be in a trance, and this behavior apparently is related to the death feigning or playing possum seen in some other animal species.

THE SPITTIN' IMAGE

When the young white-breasteds hatch, they are blind and naked, like other songbirds. In a week, they reach the gawky stage, and by the time they are ready to fledge, at the age of about two weeks, they look like their parents.

Though they cannot fly very well when they leave the nest, they are master climbers—up, down or any which way.

For a couple of weeks, the parents continue to feed them nearly all the food they get, but gradually the youngsters learn to find food for themselves. Stretching one foot forward and the other backward, they hitch down tree trunks, headfirst. Unlike woodpeckers, which use their stiff tail on tree trunks as a kind of camp stool, the nuthatch holds on only with its strong claws. A long tail would only get in the way.

Staying close to their parents, the young nuthatches work their way down tree trunks with short, jerky hops, making abrupt starts and stops as they poke into bark crevices searching for insects and their eggs and larvae. Going from the top to the bottom of the tree, they apparently find food overlooked by woodpeckers and brown creepers, which work from the bottom up.

Their menu includes caterpillars, beetles, spiders, plant lice, cankerworms, flies, and gypsy moth and tent caterpillar larvae, and a number of other forest pests.

I've always thought nuthatches look odd when they aren't clinging to a tree trunk, but occasionally they get to the bottom and continue foraging on the ground, hopping along like blue-gray frogs. Here they find nuts like acorns and hickory nuts, which they wedge into a cranny and bang with their bill until the shells open.

The youngsters also learn one of their parents' favorite pastimes —stashing food. Insects and nutmeats are wedged into caches in tree trunks and stored behind loose bark for a rainy day. These tidbits might come in handy if an ice storm or wet, clinging snow hampers the birds' usual gleaning, but they are more often eaten by the squirrels and house sparrows that find them.

At day's end, the nuthatch family roosts close to one another. During these warm days of summer and autumn, the birds find a projecting branch and cling to it overnight—upside down, naturally.

After about a month's apprenticeship, the nuthatch chicks become independent and no longer stay close to the parents, though the family remains loosely together until about the end of November. At that time, some of the brood may get the wanderlust and take off for parts unknown. Some of their siblings may stick around a bit longer, but they don't have an attachment to the territory as their parents do, and they, too, gradually drift on.

AT HOME IN THE SNOW

White-breasted nuthatches are permanent residents within their range, and by the time cold weather settles in, winter feeding territories, about the same size as breeding territories, have been established. After the young leave, the adults maintain a loose pair bond throughout the winter months.

When cold weather arrives, the white-breasteds show a renewed interest in the suet feeder.

Nuthatches also enjoy commercial bird cakes with a suet or peanut butter base.

This time of year is when nuthatches are most visible. With the leaves off the trees, it's easy to see them making their way down and around the trunks.

Though they never completely desert our feeding station during the nesting cycle, when cold weather arrives they show a renewed interest in our offerings and spend a lot more time at our suet and sunflower seed feeders.

How much they eat at the moment and how much they stash is hard to tell, but I suspect much of what they take is put into storage. Flying to our tree-trunk suet feeder, always approaching it from the top, the nuthatch hacks off a pea-sized chunk and eats it on the spot or, if there are other birds competing for a place at the suet, flies off with it.

The white-breasted enjoys our hanging sunflower seed feeder, too, clinging to the little perches with all the agility of a chickadee. It takes one seed and then flies to a nearby branch or trunk to open it. The seed is wedged into a crevice in the bark and cracked open with quick thrusts of the bird's long, slender bill. Then it's back to the feeder for another and another and another, though sometimes the little gnome tosses out six or ten seeds before finding the right one.

The nuthatches don't alter their tempo even if we happen to be there filling the feeders, or, in good weather, watering the garden or having lunch outdoors. Human activity doesn't seem to bother them. In fact, like chickadees, nuthatches are easily tamed. It's not difficult, for example, to get them to take sunflower seeds from your hand. After that, they may get quite bold, demanding and discerning. "They know perfectly well the difference in the size of the food," remarked Francis Zirrer, who had tame nuthatches at his Hayward, Wisconsin, home. "They will come, pick up the first piece, but seeing a larger piece will pause a little, drop the first one and take the larger." If the feeders are empty, "they will come to the window, or visit the woodland dweller at his place in the woods where he works at his winter supply of fuel, often a considerable distance from home; and there is usually no rest until he returns to the cabin and fills the bird table with a fresh supply of food." And, Zirrer claimed, "They become so used to a certain person and his call that they will, if within hearing distance, come when called and follow their human friend long distances through the woods. Of course, it is advisable to carry something in the pockets, which one used to such things usually does," he admitted.

With or without handouts from us, the nuthatch pair spend most of the winter's day foraging in their feeding territory. On our daily walk, we generally see only one nuthatch at a time, but it's obvious it isn't really alone. We can hear the pair's little calls to one another, their way of keeping in touch.

Recently, Hugh McIsaac, a Cornell University biology graduate, found that these intrapair calls duplicate the sound of creaking trees. In comparing sonograms of the calls nuthatch pairs use to keep in touch with the creaking of trees, McIsaac discovered that in length, harmonics, frequency range and average maximum and minimum frequency, they were the same. No doubt a predator would ignore such a common woodland noise rather than being alerted by a conspicuous bird call. There were a number of other theories put forth as to why a nuthatch's voice has this trait, including one of McIsaac's own explanations: just coincidence. In any case, this is the first known instance of a bird mimicking a plant sound.

"When, drifting through the woodland, they meet and feed in close proximity, they exchange salutations back and forth with their soft, conversational *hit, hit,*" wrote Winsor Tyler many years ago. The chickadees and brown creepers, and sometimes a downy woodpecker, often join them for a time searching for food in the same trees "until the more restless birds flit onward and leave the nuthatches alone again."

At dusk, the nuthatches settle into individual roosts for the night, but unlike their summer open-air sleeping quarters, their winter bedrooms are sheltered tree cavities.

SUET AND SUNFLOWER SEEDS WILL BRING THEM TO THE BACKYARD

If you live in an area where you can attract chickadees and downy woodpeckers to your feeding stations, you'll surely have nuthatches as well. Their favorite backyard treats are sunflower seeds and suet. They work on the suet in much the same manner as do the woodpeckers.

If you have large shade trees on your property, you have a better chance of keeping nuthatches happy. If you're very, very lucky, they might nest in a natural tree cavity in your backyard or in a large birdhouse, like a wood duck or flicker house. Try covering the house with bark and mount it at least 15 feet above the ground on a tree trunk.

Urban wildlife authority Dick DeGraaf says that you can also create a cavity by what he calls "stub-pruning." This is done by cutting off a 3- or 4-inch-diameter limb about 4–5 inches from the trunk. It rots out before it can heal over, creating an ideal nesting cavity.

The upside-down bird often finds food that other species miss on their way up the tree trunk.

LOOK-ALIKE COUSINS

Though there are 21 other nuthatch species in the world, the white-breasted has only three North American cousins.

The red-breasted nuthatch, *Sitta canadensis,* is a snappy-looking little fellow with a spunkier personality than the earnest white-breasted. Smaller (4½ inches long), but with the same short legs, large head, broad shoulders and long, slender bill, the red-breasted is the only North American nuthatch with a striking black streak through the eye topped by a white eyebrow stripe. It is a northern bird, found in coniferous forests in southern and western Canada, the western United States, the northern Great Lakes area and New England. In winter, it usually migrates farther south.

The smaller red-breasted nuthatch is a bird of northern coniferous forests.

The brown-headed nuthatch, *Sitta pusilla,* occurs only in the southeastern states. It is tiny, only 3½ inches long, with a soft, twittering call that is unlike that of other eastern nuthatches.

The western counterpart of the brown-headed is the pygmy nuthatch, *Sitta pygmaea.* It looks the same, except for a somewhat grayer cap, and even sounds the same. It is found in the pinelands of the West.

K. P. H.

WHITE-BREASTED NUTHATCH FACTS

Description: A small, stocky blue-gray bird that is typically seen hitching down tree trunks headfirst. Stub-tailed, short-necked, broad-shouldered, the white-breasted has a black cap and nape and a somewhat long, thin bill.

Habitat: Deciduous woodlands. It especially likes old trees with big trunks. Common visitor to backyards with feeding stations that offer suet and/or sunflower seeds.

Nest and Eggs: In natural tree cavity, old woodpecker hole or large birdhouse, especially one covered with bark. Inside, the nest is built of bark shreds, grasses, twigs, fur and hair, if available. May lay 5–9, but usually 8, white eggs, heavily spotted with brown or lavender.

Food: Insects, including caterpillars, beetles and spiders, and mast such as acorns and hickory nuts. Also enjoys suet and sunflower seeds.

Life Span: If it survives its first year, average expectancy in the wild is probably 2 or 3 years. Records of banded wild nuthatches show at least one that reached the age of 7½ years, another 8 years, one 9 years, and one that lived to be nearly 10.

Song: Distinctive and easily recognized. A matter-of-fact *yank, yank* or the softer *hit, hit, hit* are the calls most commonly heard.

One of the northern finches, the redpoll periodically invades U.S. feeding stations when there is a scarcity of its natural foods in the Far North.

CHAPTER ELEVEN

Other Common Backyard Birds

Selecting the 10 most popular backyard bird species in the United States was difficult. We conducted surveys around the country to see which birds were considered the most popular in various regions. No two lists were the same.

After much thought, we settled on the 10 we believe to be the most popular in the greatest number of backyards in the United States. They are the 10 birds treated in earlier chapters. At the end of each chapter, we listed similar species and regional equivalents. In most cases, they are related to the bird in the chapter; they may or may not live in the same regions. By doing this, we included most of America's favorite backyard birds, but not all.

We are giving space here to all those birds which are common backyard species in some region of the United States, but were not mentioned earlier.

THE FINCH FAMILY

In North America, the bird family with the largest number of species is the finch family. It includes buntings, cardinals, crossbills, dickcissel, finches, goldfinches, rosy finches, grosbeaks, juncos, pyrrhuloxia, redpolls, siskins, sparrows and towhees. Several in this huge family have been mentioned before. Here are some others:

Redpolls

It's considered a vintage year when the common redpolls, *Carduelis flammea,* appear at our winter feeding station. These northern finches with the conspicuous red foreheads, black chins, pink breasts and brown-streaked backs and sides are voracious eaters of Niger (thistle) seed. Competing with other kinds of finches, the redpolls literally fight for positions on both the Niger and sunflower seed cylinders. We had at least 75 redpolls at our feeders every day for several weeks a couple of winters ago. Only a few have appeared from time to time during subsequent winters. Almost fearless of humans, the redpolls chatter constantly as they eat, even when we approach to fill the feeders. Apparently, a scarcity of natural foods in the Far North causes the periodic invasions of these fascinating birds.

The white-crowned sparrow, shown here, and its close cousin the white-throated, are common backyard species throughout the continent.

The pine siskins' love for seed, combined with a feisty personality, results in constant threats and fights.

Pine Siskins

Much of what has already been said about redpolls can be said for pine siskins, *Carduelis pinus*. Their appearance at winter feeding stations is also an event, one which can last for months during severe winters. Their fondness for Niger and sunflower seeds, plus their feisty personalities, results in constant threats and fights with each other as well as other finches. Pine siskins resemble the heavily striped redpolls, but lack any red. Instead, they carry bright yellow wing bars. Often traveling companions, pine siskins and redpolls are apt to appear and disappear at the feeders on the same days.

Sparrows

Every backyard in America has sparrows of some kind. In those yards where there are great numbers of the so-called pretty birds or desirable species, the sparrows are often unwelcome visitors. In other yards, sparrows are greatly appreciated, particularly when they are the only birds in the yard.

Perhaps the most popular and widespread member of this family is the song sparrow, *Melospiza melodia*, a small brown bird with heavy stripes on its back, breast and face. The breast also has a large central dot. The most distinguishing characteristic of the song

Perhaps the most popular and widespread member of the sparrow family is the song sparrow, a bird at home in many habitats.

A winter-only resident in the U.S., the tree sparrow is a common feeding-station visitor across most of the North.

sparrow, however, is its song. Naturalist Robert M. McClung claimed that song sparrows have been heard singing almost constantly for nine hours a day—more than 2,000 separate songs! It is a very melodious, multifaceted sound which was described by Thoreau as *"Maids! maids! maids! hang up your teakettle-ettle-ettle."* And as human accents vary with the region, so too does the song of this sparrow.

A bird at home in many habitats, the song sparrow is found in thickets, forest edges, brushy areas, hedgerows and even on beaches. Its 31 subspecies inhabit almost all areas of North America, from the Aleutian Islands in Alaska to the southern tip of Florida.

The song sparrow builds a well-hidden nest on the ground under tufts of grass or brush, or sometimes in low brush, or, on rare occasions, in trees up to 12 feet. Inside the nesting cup of grasses, weed stems and bark fibers, song sparrows lay three to five greenish-white, heavily spotted eggs. Incubation by the female requires 12–13 days for hatching. The pair usually has two broods a year, sometimes three.

Song sparrows eat insects in the summer and seeds and wild fruits in the winter. At backyard feeding stations, they are attracted to cracked corn and a variety of seeds such as red and white millet.

Another true sparrow which frequents backyards is the chipping sparrow, *Spizella passerina,* a small bird with a reddish cap, white stripe above the eye, black eye streak and pale grayish underparts. A summer-only resident in the North, the chipping sparrow's insectlike trill can be heard from the evergreens where it nests in open woodlands, forest edges, farmlands, suburban backyards and parks.

Much like the chippy in appearance, but a little larger and with a black spot in the middle of its gray breast, is the American tree sparrow, *Spizella arborea.* This winter resident in the United States is a popular feeding-station visitor across most of the North. It leaves the lower 48 states for its Canadian and Alaskan nesting grounds in March and April.

Both white-throated, *Zonotrichia albicollis,* and white-crowned, *Zonotrichia leucophrys,* sparrows are common backyard species throughout much of the continent, particularly in the East and Midwest during winter. Their western counterpart, the golden-crowned,

This nondescript female house sparrow and her black-bibbed mate are considered pest species in most neighborhoods.

Zonotrichia atricapilla, visits backyards along the Pacific Coast. Just as their names indicate, these large sparrows have white and gold where indicated. All three have lovely songs, the most famous being the white-throat's *Old Sam, peabody-peabody-peabody.* In Canada, they believe the bird says, *Oh sweet, Canada-Canada-Canada.*

Undoubtedly the most common of the sparrowlike birds in a great many backyards is actually a weaverbird known as the house sparrow or English sparrow, *Passer domesticus.* As its scientific name indicates, this European import has done well in the human environment, thriving when horses provided our transportation. The grains and straw seeds associated with horses were quite beneficial to this alien. Today, it is considered an undesirable pest in most neighborhoods. Males have a dapper black bib, reddish back and head, with whitish-gray underparts. Females are rather nondescript brownish-gray birds.

Though also not a sparrow, the dark-eyed junco or snowbird, *Junco hyemalis,* is a sparrowlike creature that is neatly dressed in slate-colored gray above and snow white below, including white outer tail feathers. One of the first migrants to return to the feeding station in the fall and usually the last to leave in the spring, the junco is a quiet, well-mannered little fellow that loves cracked corn as well as both red and white millet. Common across most of the United States during winter, it migrates north in spring to nest in the coniferous forests of the border states, Canada and Alaska.

The first migrant to return to the feeding station in the fall and the last to leave in the spring is the dark-eyed junco.

Towhees

For many people, springtime in the East or Midwest is not complete without the friendly *DRINK-your teeeeee!* song of the rufous-sided towhee, *Pipilo erythrophthalmus*. Its sweet *toe-WHEE!* is also a delightful sound heard from the hedgerow as the bird scratches in the dry leaves for bugs and beetles. Towhees are smaller and more slender than robins; the sexes are somewhat different but both attractive in appearance. The male's head and upperparts are jet black, sides robin-red, belly white. He flashes large white patches in his tail in flight. The female is a rich brown where the male is black. They make a handsome pair.

Rufous-sideds are found across the southern half of the United States year-round, but many migrate north in the spring all the way

Calling its name as it scratches for bugs in dry leaves, the towhee is a delightful bird to have as a backyard resident.

into southern Canada. They are a common winter feeding-station bird in the South. I have photographed them eating at seed trays in Florida and Georgia. They are a delightful bird whenever they frequent a backyard, bringing cheerful song and interesting habits with them. The rufous-sided is the only towhee in the East, but the West is blessed with three more species: the green-tailed of the high country and Northwest; the brown, located in the desert Southwest; and Abert's, of the Southwest and Far West. All towhees are prospective backyard visitors where low, brushy cover gives them a feeling of safety.

SUBFAMILY ICTERINAE

Another major group of birds throughout North America are the 22 species of the Icterinae subfamily. These include the well-known blackbirds, grackles, orioles, meadowlarks, cowbirds and the bobolink. The habitat requirements for most of these are rural or farmland, but these birds also find their way to many suburban backyards.

The best known of all the blackbirds, the red-winged is thought to be the most numerous bird in North America.

Blackbirds

The best-known bird of this family is the red-winged blackbird, *Agelaius phoeniceus,* thought to be the most numerous bird in North America. We know it well in our Wisconsin backyard and look forward to the first *con-ka-reee* of spring, which is heard in early to mid-March. Redwings nest in the little wetland at the west end of our lake. So close are we to their nesting grounds that the males dash from their territories in the cattails to our feeders, grab a couple of seeds, and then hurry back to the marsh again. It is interesting that the very same jet-black males with scarlet-and-yellow shoulder patches who fight each other with vengeance in the marsh quietly share positions on the feeders at our patio only a few hundred yards away. Females, on the other hand, don't visit our feeders. This is an all-male club, and the only birds at our feeders which resemble the brown-striped females are the immature males that are permitted to join the club in late summer.

Cowbirds

A traveling companion of the redwings during migration is the brown-headed cowbird, *Molothrus ater,* the species that lays its eggs in the nests of other birds. Common throughout most of the continent, cowbirds parasitize other species all across the continent from British Columbia to the Gulf of Mexico. As with most members of the troupial family, the cowbird sexes are so different in appearance that they do not look like they belong together. The male cowbird has a brown head; its body is all-black, while the female is simply gray all over. We call her the "gray lady," as she stalks around, eyeing prospective nests in which to lay her eggs. The bronzed cowbird, *Molothrus aeneus,* is the brown-headed's southwestern counterpart.

Grackles

Certainly anything but a favorite backyard bird, but one that must be mentioned, is the common grackle, *Quiscalus quiscula,* a large, iridescent black bird with purple, bronze or greenish casts, and a very long, keel-shaped tail. Congregating in unusually large flocks with other members of the troupial family, grackles have become

The brown-headed cowbird lays its eggs in the nests of other birds. This rare photograph shows a female laying her egg in the nest of a red-eyed vireo.

infamous for their habit of roosting by the thousands, sometimes the millions, from fall through winter and into early spring. Their annoying *check, check, check* call plus the droppings they leave has made grackles very unpopular backyard visitors. Mostly an eastern species, the common's larger southern and midwestern relatives are the boat-tailed grackle, *Quiscalus major,* and its more western cousin, the great-tailed, *Quiscalus mexicanus*.

Young northern orioles peeking from their well-hidden pouchlike nest are fed by their brightly colored father.

Orioles

Who doesn't thrill to the flash of brilliant orange and the liquid song of the northern oriole, *Icterus galbula?* Once known as the Baltimore oriole for the male's orange-and-black colors, the same ones chosen by the first Baron of Baltimore for his livery and coat of arms, the bird was renamed "northern" by the American Ornithologists' Union when they lumped it with a western oriole formerly named Bullock's oriole. Regardless of what we call it, the oriole is an extremely popular backyard species because of the male's bright, showy colors (the female is much duller) and loud, clear, flutelike whistle. The female oriole's nest is a deep pouch woven of plant fibers, attached to a drooping branch 6–60 feet above the ground. It is so well hidden in the leaves that we usually don't find it until the leaves have dropped and the birds have long since gone south. The northern oriole winters in the Gulf states and into Mexico, but nests in a great many of the lower 48 states and southern Canada. Though orioles nest in our yard, we don't get to see them up close unless they come to the birdbath or eat oranges at our feeders. We bait them by impaling half an orange on a nail against a tree trunk. It usually takes only a few hours for an oriole (usually a male) to find the orange. They will continue to eat oranges until early July, and then for some reason, they ignore them during the balance of their stay. The northern's cousin, the orchard oriole, is a dark orange bird that lives only in the East. Their western relatives, the Scott's, Audubon's, hooded, and Altamira, are all beautifully colored birds that are likely visitors to backyards in the regions in which they live.

STARLING

Probably the most unwanted backyard visitor in North America is the European starling, whose scientific name, *Sturnus vulgaris,* shows that it was unpopular long before it was introduced into the United States in 1890. A dominant species among most other songbirds, the starling is famous for chasing more desirable birds away from nesting cavities and feeding stations. Starlings are identified by their long, pointed yellow bills, short tails and overall iridescent black bodies with purple and greenish gloss during summer. Their

Introduced to North America in 1890, the European starling is probably the most unwanted backyard bird.

winter plumages are quite speckled with white or light tan spots and a grayish-colored bill. I know people who are familiar with the starling's summer garb, but think they are looking at another species in winter. A mimic almost as talented as the mockingbird, the starling has a large repertoire of sounds ranging from whistles and squawks to chatters, creaks and chips. It can imitate dozens of other birds' songs.

SWALLOW FAMILY

These sleek, aerial acrobats are among our most beloved birds. In North America, the swallow family includes martins and 11 species of swallows. Several have adapted quite well to human habitation and now return to villages and suburbs in search of nesting sites. Barn swallows and purple martins are the best examples. Because all members of this family depend heavily on insects as food, they must migrate south to more favorable climates during winter months. They return to the North on approximately the same date each year. Swallows usually travel together in huge flocks.

Swallows

The most famous of the swallows of North America are those that return to the Mission of San Juan Capistrano, California, on or about March 19 each year. They are cliff swallows, *Hirundo pyrrhonota,* birds that build colonies of little adobe globes under the eaves of buildings. Common throughout most of the continent, cliff swallows differ in appearance from other swallows by their dark back, light forehead and rusty rump and throat. Their natural nesting sites are under cliffs, near water.

The most water-oriented of the group is the tree swallow, *Tachycineta bicolor,* with steely blue-green-black upperparts and white

The most famous swallows in North America are the cliff swallows that return to Capistrano every March.

Like other members of their family, these tree swallows migrate in large flocks.

underparts. Tree swallows build solitary nests in tree cavities (they will accept birdhouses), usually near or over water. They are also known to use old woodpecker cavities in fenceposts, rural mailboxes, and holes in buildings. They are rather tame and will not hesitate to raise their families in backyards if conditions are right. The tree swallow's western counterpart is the violet-green swallow, *Tachycineta thalassina,* a near look-alike but with more white on its flanks and rump.

The swallow that most often nests near people is the barn swallow, *Hirundo rustica,* the only member of the clan with a forked tail and glossy blue back, light rufous underparts and a darker throat.

Often in colonies, barn swallows nest around many kinds of structures, especially in barns, under bridges, on wharves and on boathouses. They plaster their mud nests to the beams of the structures and typically line them profusely with white chicken feathers. These graceful fliers are usually a much-appreciated summer resident anywhere they choose to live.

Purple Martin

More money has been spent by disappointed backyard owners to attract purple martins than any other bird species. But purple martins, *Progne subis,* are fickle birds and will nest only where conditions are exactly right, and then only if they want to. Famous for consuming great numbers of mosquitoes, purple martins nest in dense colonies, usually in multiple-room houses set on poles 15–20 feet above the ground. Especially in the South, they will also nest

Barn swallows plaster their mud nests to beams in barns and other structures and usually line them profusely with white chicken feathers.

Usually nesting in multiple-room houses like this one in Helenville, Wisconsin, purple martins enjoy the steel rods placed there for their use.

Purple martins will also nest in hollowed gourds hung in clusters on poles, especially in the South.

in hollowed gourds with two-inch holes cut in the sides and hung in clusters on poles. Males arrive on the northern nesting grounds before the females. These so-called scouts check out the old martin houses and investigate new ones. Actual nesting sites are selected after the females arrive a week or so later. If you hope to attract martins, place the nesting houses in an open area, preferably near water, and where there are also utility wires upon which the birds can perch. In the absence of utility wires, steel rods extending from the birdhouse will serve the same purpose. If there are already colonies of purple martins in the immediate area, chances of attracting these wonderful birds are greatly increased.

HUMMINGBIRD FAMILY

Hummingbirds get their family name from the noise made as they beat insectlike wings in flight. They range from the smallest bird in the world, the 2¼-inch bee hummingbird in Cuba (for which we once searched in vain), to the 8½-inch-long giant hummingbird of the South American Andes (which we found and photographed in Ecuador). Of the 319 species in the world, only 19 have been recorded in the United States, of which only 8 species get much beyond the Mexican border. Seven of those are strictly western species, leaving only one, the ruby-throated, *Archilochus colubris,* in the East. This 3–3½-inch mite has a long bill, metallic green plumage above and dull white below. The male has a metallic red throat, which in some lights appears black; the female's throat is gray. Unlike other birds, hummingbirds can fly in any direction at will, including backward. In fact, their courtship ritual includes a great many aerial gyrations by the male. Most hummingbirds must migrate south before cold weather takes their food supplies of nectar and insects. The ruby-throated's migration is a long one for a bird so small. Some individuals fly from southern Canada to the Gulf of Mexico, where they cross 600 miles of water and then continue to their wintering grounds in Central America. Those that survive must cross the Gulf twice every year.

The ruby-throated's nest is typical of most hummingbirds. It is a tiny, one-inch cup of plant down and fibers, attached with spider

silk to a twig or small branch. The two pure-white eggs look like
Navy beans. Only the female incubates. In fact, the male takes no
part at all in the nesting activity, not even in feeding the young. In
Michigan, a female rubythroat was observed alternately feeding a
youngster in one nest and incubating two eggs in another nest only
four feet away. Both nests successfully fledged young.

Rubythroats, like all hummingbirds in the United States, can be
enticed to drink sugar water from a feeder. They are more likely to
come to a feeder in areas where there is a limited supply of natural
nectar. In northern Wisconsin, Michigan and Minnesota for example, where ruby-throated hummingbirds commonly nest, there are
few flowers to provide an abundance of nectar, and thus red-colored
sugar water is very successful in attracting hummers to cottage windows throughout the region.

*The ruby-throated hummingbird's nest is a tiny one-inch cup of plant
down and fibers, attached with spider silk to a twig or small branch.*

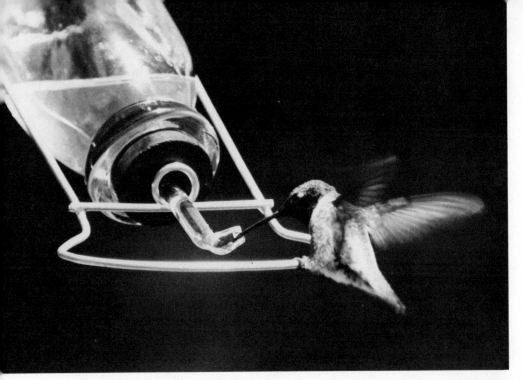

Most of the 19 species of hummingbirds in the United States can be lured to sugar water feeders, as was this black-chinned in Arizona.

The rubythroat's western counterpart is the broad-tailed hummingbird, *Selasphorus platycercus,* a similar bird that nests in the Rockies. I remember how easy it was to attract broadtails to sugar-water feeders in the Estes Park, Colorado area. I also remember the unique, shrill metallic whistling of their wings as they flew to and from the feeders.

Most of the other western hummingbirds can be seen at one time or another during the year in the Huachuca Mountains of southeastern Arizona. At The Nature Conservancy's Mile-Hi Ranch in Ramsey Canyon, 12 species of hummingbirds are fed during the course of the year. The locally common western species not already mentioned include the black-chinned, Costa's, Anna's, rufous, Allen's, Calliope, magnificent, blue-throated and broad-billed. All can be enticed to the backyards of their regions with sugar water.

Appendix

FOOD, COVER AND NESTING
PREFERENCES FOR NORTHEASTERN
BACKYARD BIRDS

From *A Manual for the Northeast:*

*Trees, Shrubs, and Vines
for Attracting Birds*

BY

RICHARD M. DEGRAAF

AND

GRETCHEN M. WITMAN

UNIVERSITY OF MASSACHUSETTS PRESS
1979

AMERICAN ROBIN

Tree or Plant	Food	Cover	Nesting
Balsam Fir		X	X
Maples	S	X	X
Serviceberries*	F		
Common Hackberry*	F		
Flowering Dogwood*	F		X
Common Persimmon*	F		
Hollies*	F	X	X
Eastern Red Cedar*	F	X	X
Eastern Larch		X	X
Apples*	F	X	X
Mulberries*	F		
Tupelo*	F		
Spruces		X	X
Eastern White Pine		X	X
Pin Cherry*	F		
Black Cherry*	F		X
Common Chokecherry*	F		
Oaks			X
Common Sassafras*	F		
American Mountain-ash*	F		
Northern White Cedar	S	X	X
Eastern Hemlock		X	X
American Elm			X
Red Chokeberry	F		
Japanese Barberry	F		
European Barberry	F		
Dogwoods*	F	X	
Hawthorns	F	X	X
Russian Olive*	F		
Autumn Olive*	F	X	
Huckleberries	F	X	X
Common Juniper*	F		
Common Spicebush	F		
Honeysuckles*	F		
Scarlet Firethorn*	F		
Buckthorns	F		
Sumacs*	F		
Gooseberries*	F	X	X
Roses	F		
Brambles*	F		
Elders	F	X	

Tree or Plant	Food	Cover	Nesting
Common Snowberry	F		
Coralberry*	F		
Yews	F	X	X
Blueberries*	F		
Viburnums	F		
American Bittersweet	F		
Common Moonseed	F		
Virginia Creeper*	F		
Cat Greenbrier*	F		
Common Greenbrier*	F		
Grapes*	F		

* Preferred food. (F, fruit; S, seed.)

BLACK-CAPPED CHICKADEE

Tree or Plant	Food	Cover	Nesting
Balsam Fir	S	X	
Birches	S	X	X (Cavity)
American Beech	F		
Butternut*	F		
American Sweetgum	S		
Spruces	S	X	X (Cavity)
Pitch Pine*	S	X	X (Cavity)
Eastern White Pine*	S	X	X (Cavity)
Bigtooth Aspen		X	X (Cavity)
Quaking Aspen		X	X (Cavity)
Eastern Hemlock	S		
American Elm	S	X	X (Cavity)
Serviceberries	F		
Red Chokeberry	F		
Black Chokeberry	F		
Autumn Olive	F		
Northern Bayberry	F		
Blueberries	F		
Virginia Creeper	F		
Poison Ivy*	F		

* Preferred food. (F, fruit; S, seed.)

MOCKINGBIRD

Tree or Plant	Food	Cover	Nesting
Serviceberries	F		
Common Hackberry*	F		
Flowering Dogwood*	F		
Common Persimmon*	F		
Hollies*	F	X	X
Eastern Red Cedar*	F	X	X
Apples	F	X	X
Mulberries*	F		
Tupelo*	F		
American Hop-hornbeam	F		
Spruces		X	X
Pin Cherry	F		
Black Cherry*	F		
Common Chokecherry	F		
Common Sassafras	F		
Japanese Barberry*	F	X	
European Barberry	F		
Dogwoods	F	X	
Hawthorns	F	X	X
Russian Olive	F	X	X
Autumn Olive*	F	X	
Huckleberries	F	X	X
Common Juniper	F		
Honeysuckles	F	X	X
Northern Bayberry	F		
Scarlet Firethorn*	F		
Buckthorns*	F		
Sumacs*	F		
Gooseberries*	F	X	X
Roses*	F	X	X
Brambles*	F	X	X
Elders*	F	X	X
Yews	F	X	X
Viburnums	F		
American Bittersweet	F		
Virginia Creeper*	F		
Cat Greenbrier*	F	X	X
Common Greenbrier*	F	X	X
Poison Ivy*	F		

Tree or Plant	Food	Cover	Nesting
Grapes*	F	X	X
White Spruce			X
White Fir			X
Multiflora Rose*	F	X	X

* Preferred food. (F, fruit; S, seed.)

CARDINAL

Tree or Plant	Food	Cover	Nesting
Maples	S		
Serviceberries	F		
Birches	S		
American Hornbeam*	F		
Hickories*	F		
Common Hackberry*	F		
Flowering Dogwood*	F		
Ashes*	S		
Hollies	F	X	X
Eastern Black Walnut*	F		
Eastern Red Cedar	F	X	X
American Sweetgum*	S		
Yellow Poplar*	S		
Apples	F		X
Mulberries*	F		
Eastern White Pine*	S	X	X
Pin Cherry	F		
Black Cherry*	F		
Common Chokecherry	F		
Oaks	F		
American Elm	S		
Devil's Walkingstick	F	X	X
Japanese Barberry	F		
Dogwoods*	F	X	
Hawthorns	F	X	X
Russian Olive	F		
Autumn Olive*	F	X	
Witch-hazel	S		
Common Spicebush	F		
Scarlet Firethorn	F		
Sumacs*	F		
Roses	F	X	X

(continued)

(Cardinal continued)

Tree or Plant	Food	Cover	Nesting
Brambles*	F	X	X
Elders	F	X	
Coralberry	F	X	
Blueberries	F		
Viburnums	F		
American Bittersweet	F		
Cat Greenbrier	F	X	X
Common Greenbrier	F	X	X
Grapes*	F	X	X
Multiflora Rose	F	X	X

* Preferred food. (F, food; S, seed.)

MOURNING DOVE

Tree or Plant	Food	Cover	Nesting
Balsam Fir		X	X
Serviceberries	F		
Ashes		X	X
Eastern Red Cedar	F		
American Sweetgum*	S		
Spruces	S	X	X
Pitch Pine	S	X	X
Eastern White Pine*	S	X	X
Oaks	F		
Eastern Hemlock		X	X
Alders	S		
Sweetfern	F		
Russian Olive	F	X	X
Autumn Olive	F	X	
Huckleberries	F	X	
Hollies	F		
Gooseberries	F		
Elders	F	X	
Blueberries	F	X	
Ampelopsis	F		
Grapes	F		
White Fir			X
White Spruce			X

* Preferred food. (F, food; S, seed.)

AMERICAN GOLDFINCH

Tree or Plant	Food	Cover	Nesting
Maples	S	X	X
Serviceberries	F		
Birches*	S,BD		
American Hornbeam*	F		
American Sweetgum*	S		
Yellow Poplar	S		
Mulberries*	F		
Spruces	S	X	
Pitch Pine	S		
Eastern White Pine	S		
Pin Cherry	F		
Black Cherry	F		
Common Chokecherry	F		
Eastern Hemlock*	S		
American Elm*	S,BD		
Alders*	S		
Honeysuckles*	F		
Roses	F		
Willows		X	X (pussy)
Elders		X	X
Spireas			X
Common Trumpet Creeper	S		
Grapes			X
Red-osier Dogwood			X
Hardhack			X

* Preferred food. (F, fruit; S, seeds; BD, buds.)

DOWNY WOODPECKER

Tree or Plant	Food	Cover	Nesting
Serviceberries	F		
Birches		X	X (Cavity)
Flowering Dogwood	F		
American Beech	F		
Eastern Black Walnut*	F		
Apples	F,S		
Mulberries	F		
Tupelo	F		
American Hop-hornbeam	F		

(continued)

(Downy Woodpecker continued)

Tree or Plant	Food	Cover	Nesting
Spruces	S	X	X (Cavity)
Bigtooth Aspen		X	X (Cavity)
Quaking Aspen		X	X (Cavity)
Pin Cherry	F		
Black Cherry	F		
Common Chokecherry	F		
Oaks	F		
American Elm		X	X (Cavity)
Dogwoods*	F		
Common Juniper	F		
Northern Bayberry	F		
Buckthorns	F		
Sumacs	F		
Virginia Creeper	F		
Poison Ivy*	F		

* Preferred food. (F, fruit; S, seed.)

HOUSE WREN

Tree or Plant	Food	Cover	Nesting
Any low cavity in shrubbery shaded by larger trees.			X

BLUE JAY

Tree or Plant	Food	Cover	Nesting
Balsam Fir	S	X	X
Serviceberries	F		
Birches	S		
Hickories	F		
American Beech*	F		
Eastern Black Walnut*	F		
Eastern Larch		X	X
Apples	F,S	X	X
Mulberries*	F		
Tupelo	F		

Tree or Plant	Food	Cover	Nesting
Spruces		X	X
Eastern White Pine		X	X
Pin Cherry	F		
Black Cherry*	F		
Common Chokecherry	F		
Oaks*	F		
Eastern Hemlock		X	X
Devil's Walkingstick	F	X	
Eastern Chinkapin	F		
American Hazel*	F		
Beaked Filbert*	F		
Hawthorns	F		X
Huckleberries*	F		
Scarlet Firethorn	F		
Sumacs	F		
Brambles*	F		
Elders	F	X	
Blueberries*	F		
Grapes	F		
Maples			X

* Preferred food. (F, fruit; S, seed.)

WHITE-BREASTED NUTHATCH

Tree or Plant	Food	Cover	Nesting
Balsam Fir	S	X	
Birches	S	X	X (Cavity)
Hickories*	F		
American Beech*	F		
Butternut*	F		
Pitch Pine*	S	X	X (Cavity)
Eastern White Pine*	S	X	X (Cavity)
Oaks	F		
American Mountain-ash	F		
American Elm		X	X (Cavity)
Elders	F		
Virginia Creeper	F		

* Preferred food. (F, fruit; S, seed.)

GLOSSARY

Altricial: Birds which usually hatch blind, naked and helpless, totally dependent on their parents for food and care. The opposite of precocial.

Brood: *Noun:* The chicks hatched from a single set of eggs. *Verb:* To cover with the body and wings. Brooding provides warmth to young nestlings which are not yet capable of regulating their body temperatures, and on hot days protects them from the hot sun. It also shelters them from rain.

Brood Patch, or Incubation Patch: A bare spot that appears during the breeding season on the lower breast of those adult birds that are responsible for incubating eggs. Before incubation begins, the down and feathers drop from this area. This bare area swells, or thickens, and develops a rich supply of blood vessels near the skin surface. When sitting on eggs, the bird keeps this area pressed against them. Its body warmth is thereby transferred to the eggs, keeping them at an even incubation temperature of about 93 degrees Fahrenheit.

Call: A note or notes that are not a "song." Generally a call is only one note, sometimes two. Birds have various calls and notes, one of the more common being the "alarm" note which warns of danger.

Clutch: The total number of eggs produced by a bird during a single nesting. A set of eggs.

Contour Feathers: The outer feathers of a bird that cover the downy underlining and follow the contour, or shape, of the bird's body.

Copulation: Sexual union; coupling.

Crest: On birds, a tuft of feathers on the top of the head. The bird can raise or lower the crest at will.

Crop: An enlarged area in the esophagus which stores or partly digests food that is taken in too rapidly for the stomach to handle. In pigeons and doves, the crop produces "milk" during the breeding season from seeds eaten by the adults. This "milk" is fed by regurgitation to the young.

Display: A performance or special posture assumed by a bird to impress a potential mate, or to threaten a rival. A display might involve the spreading of feathers to show them off to their best advantage, as in the male peacock. It might be ecstatic dancing, such as that of cranes. In songbirds, it frequently involves spreading the wings and tail, often accompanied by a bow. Song usually follows or is part of display.

Down, or Down Feathers: The soft, fluffy covering that is a young bird's first plumage. In adults, the down is next to the skin, under the contour feathers, and seems to be primarily for insulation.

Drumming: A sound birds produce that sounds like drumming. Woodpeckers drum by loudly tapping a rhythm with their bills against hollow tree trunks or, sometimes, outer walls of buildings, chimneys, etc. Ruffed grouse also drum, but in a very different manner. The male grouse stands sideways on a log and drums by beating cupped wings. The drumming sound is produced when the cupped wings hit the air. In both cases, the birds' drumming serves the same purpose as songs in other birds, i.e., attraction of a mate and defense of territory.

Egg Tooth: A small, whitish, horny patch, often with a sharp projection, on top of a hatching chick's bill. It helps the young bird break out of its shell, and at the same time protects the still-soft bill. Almost all birds have an egg tooth at the time of hatching, but it disappears shortly afterward, either by falling off or by being absorbed.

Fecal Sac: A tiny, whitish sac excreted by baby birds, resembling a miniature balloon filled with white fluid. It contains the nestling's excrement. The parents remove the sacs from the nest, either by taking them away and dropping them, or eating them.

Fledge: To leave the nest.

Fledgling: A young bird that has left the nest but is still dependent on its parents.

Grit: Sand or small stone granules that some birds eat to aid the gizzard in its grinding digestion. Grit also provides birds with necessary minerals, especially calcium.

Incubation: The act whereby the adult provides body heat to eggs by sitting on them, thus promoting development of the embryo.

Juvenal: *Adjective:* Refers to a young bird's first plumage of true feathers.

Juvenile: *Noun:* One who is not an adult; one who is not sexually mature.

Molt: To acquire new plumage through the gradual process of shedding old feathers and growing new ones. All adult birds molt at least once a year, usually after the breeding season (postnuptial molt). Many species molt two times a year, some more frequently.

Nestling: A young bird still in the nest.

Pipping: The process of breaking out of an eggshell. The egg is said to be pipped when it has been punctured from the inside out by the hatching chick.

Plumage: A bird's covering of feathers.

Precocial: Birds that hatch with a downy coat, eyes fully open, and that are capable of leaving the nest within hours of hatching. Ducks, quail, pheasants and grouse are examples of precocial birds.

Predator: One who survives by killing and eating other species.

Preening: The act of grooming the feathers with the bill. In preening, the bird cleans and smooths the feathers by grasping a feather with the bill and "nibbling" it from the base to the tip, or by merely pulling the closed bill over the feather. During preening, oil is spread from the oil gland at the base of the tail throughout the body feathers.

Primary Feather: One of the main flight feathers in the wings. Primaries, usually ten on each wing, are along the wing's outer edge.

Quill: Also called the calamus. The quill is the hollow main shaft of a feather.

Raptor: A bird of prey, such as an eagle, falcon, hawk, owl or shrike.

Regurgitation: In birds, the act by which an adult bird forces up partially digested food from its crop or stomach to feed its young.

Roost: *Noun:* The place where a bird perches to rest or sleep. *Verb:* To rest or sleep on a roost.

Song: A series of notes, often melodious, that a bird produces to advertise its availability as a mate, to attract a potential mate and to defend territory. Usually produced only during the breeding season. Songs are often elaborate phrases, and are different from calls, which usually have only one or two notes.

Suet: The hard, white fat that surrounds the kidney on cattle. A favorite feeding-station food of woodpeckers, nuthatches, chickadees, titmice and starlings.

Territory: In birds, an area that the bird defends for the purpose of nesting and/or feeding.

LITERATURE CITED

Allen, Arthur A. *American Bird Biographies*. Ithaca, New York: Comstock Publishing Company, 1934.

———. *The Golden Plover and Other Birds*. Ithaca, New York: Comstock Publishing Company, 1939.

Baldwin, S. P., and Kendeigh, S. C. "Periods of Attentiveness and Inattentiveness in the Nesting Behavior of the House Wren." *Auk,* vol. XLIV, no. 2 (1927).

Bancroft, Griffing. *The White Cardinal*. New York: Coward-McCann & Geoghegan, Inc., 1973.

Bent, Arthur Cleveland. *Life Histories of North American Cardinals, Grosbeaks, Buntings, Towhees, Finches, Sparrows and Allies*. 3 vols. New York: Dover Publications, Inc., 1968.

———. *Life Histories of North American Jays, Crows and Titmice*. New York: Dover Publications, Inc., 1964.

———. *Life Histories of North American Nuthatches, Wrens, Thrashers and Their Allies*. New York: Dover Publications, Inc., 1964.

———. *Life Histories of North American Thrushes, Kinglets and Their Allies*. New York: Dover Publications, Inc., 1964.

Callahan, Philip S. *Birds and How They Function*. New York: Holiday House, 1979.

Christy, B. H. "The Cardinal: The Bird Itself." *Cardinal,* vol. 5, no. 8 (July, 1942).

DeGraaf, R. M., and Witman, G. W. *Trees, Shrubs and Vines for Attracting Birds*. Amherst: University of Massachusetts Press, 1979.

Dolton, David D. *1982 Mourning Dove Breeding Population Status.* Laurel, Maryland: U.S. Fish and Wildlife Service Office of Migratory Bird Management, 1982.

Drum, Margaret. "Territorial Studies on the Eastern Goldfinch." *Wilson Bulletin,* vol. 51, no. 2 (June, 1939).

DuBois, A. D. *Glimpses of Bird Life.* Minneapolis: T. S. Denison & Company, Inc., 1974.

Eisener, Len. *The American Robin.* Chicago: Nelson-Hall, 1976.

Grzimek, Dr. Bernhard. *Grzimek's Animal Life Encyclopedia.* Volume 7. New York: Van Nostrand Reinhold Company, 1972.

Harrison, Hal H. *American Birds in Color.* New York: Wm. H. Wise & Company, Inc., 1948.

————. *A Field Guide to Birds' Nests.* Boston: Houghton Mifflin Company, 1975.

————. *A Field Guide to Western Birds' Nests.* Boston: Houghton Mifflin Company, 1979.

Hawksley, O., and McCormack, A. P. "Doubly-Occupied Nests of the Eastern Cardinal." *Auk,* vol. 68, no. 4 (October, 1951).

Howell, Joseph C. "Notes on the Nesting Habits of the American Robin." *American Midland Naturalist,* vol. 28, no. 3, (November, 1942).

Ingold, James L. "Defense of Breeding Territories in the White-Breasted Nuthatch." *Passenger Pigeon,* vol. 43, no. 2.

Ivor, H. R. "Observations on 'Anting' by Birds." *Auk,* vol. 58, no. 3 (July 1941).

Kilham, Lawrence. "Reproductive Behavior of White-Breasted Nuthatches—II." *Auk,* vol. 89, no. 1 (January, 1972).

————. "Reproductive Behavior of White-Breasted Nuthatches." *Auk,* vol. 85, no. 3 (July, 1968).

Lawrence, Louise de Kiriline. *Black-Capped Chickadee.* Ottawa: Canadian Wildlife Service/Information Canada, 1973.

————. *A Comparative Life-History Study of Four Species of Woodpeckers.* Ann Arbor: American Ornithologists' Union, 1967.

Leopold, Aldo. *A Sand County Almanac.* New York: Oxford University Press, 1949.

Logan, Stanley. "Cardinal, *Richmondena cardinalis,* Assists in Feeding of Robins." *Auk,* vol. 68, no. 4 (October, 1951).

Longstreet, R. J. "Migration Flight of Goldfinches, Kingbirds, and Nighthawks." *Auk,* vol. 45, no. 2 (April, 1928).

Lopez, Barry. "Mighty Chickadee." *National Wildlife,* April/May, 1975.

Madson, John. *The Mourning Dove.* East Alton, Illinois: Winchester Press/Olin Corporation, 1978.

Maslowski, Steve. "Big Red Booms in Cincinnati." *National Wildlife,* December/January, 1983.

Miller, Ansel B. "Notes: Four-Brooded Cardinals." *Cardinal,* vol. 6, no. 1 (January, 1943).

Murray, Dr. J. J. "The Cardinal." *Virginia Wildlife,* October, 1958.

———. "The Carolina Chickadee." *Virginia Wildlife,* August, 1960.

———. "The Carolina Wren." *Virginia Wildlife,* January, 1959.

———. "The House Wren." *Virginia Wildlife,* May, 1959.

———. "The Mockingbird." *Virginia Wildlife,* March, 1959.

———. "The Robin." *Virginia Wildlife,* October, 1958.

Nice, Margaret. " 'Territorial Song' and Non-Territorial Behavior of Goldfinches in Ohio." *Wilson Bulletin,* vol. 51, no. 2 (June, 1939).

Nickell, P. "Studies of Habitats, Territory, and Nests of the Eastern Goldfinch." *Auk,* vol. 68, no. 4 (October, 1951).

Odum, Eugene P. "Annual Cycle of the Black-Capped Chickadee—1." *Auk,* vol. 58, no. 3 (July, 1941).

———. "Annual Cycle of the Black-Capped Chickadee." *Auk,* vol. 59, no. 4 (October, 1942).

———. "Nesting Cycle of the Black-Capped Chickadee—2." *Auk,* vol. 58, no. 4 (October, 1941).

Peterson, Roger Tory. *A Field Guide to the Birds.* 4th ed. Boston: Houghton Mifflin Company, 1980.

———. *A Field Guide to Western Birds.* Boston: Houghton Mifflin Company, 1969.

Reeves, H. M., Geis, A. D., and Kniffin, F. G. "Field Methods for Sex and Age Determination of Mourning Doves." *Mourning Dove Capture and Banding.* Washington: Bureau of Sport Fisheries and Wildlife, 1969.

Robbins, C. S., Bruun, B., and Zim, H. S. *Birds of North America.* New York: Golden Press/Western Publishing Company, 1966.

Sayre, M. W., Baskett, T. S., and Sadler, K. C. *Radiotelemetry Studies of the Mourning Dove in Missouri.* Jefferson City: The Conservation Commission of the State of Missouri, 1980.

Sayre, Roxanna. "Creatures." *Audubon,* March, 1982.

Simon, Hilda. *The Courtship of Birds.* New York: Dodd, Mead & Company, Inc., 1977.

Skutch, Alexander F. *Parent Birds and Their Young.* Austin: University of Texas Press, 1976.

Smith, Dr. Charles R. "Chickadees in Winter." *Laboratory of Ornithology Newsletter,* 1980.

Smith, H. H., Sr. "Our Friendly Mockers." *Virginia Wildlife,* March, 1958.

Snyder, L. L. " 'Anting' by the Cardinal." *Auk,* vol. 58, no. 3 (July, 1941).

Stefferud, Alfred, ed. *Birds in Our Lives.* Washington: U.S. Fish and Wildlife Service, 1966.

Terres, John K. *The Audubon Society Encyclopedia of North American Birds.* New York: Alfred A. Knopf, 1980.

Weinert, Susan J., ed. *North American Wildlife.* Pleasantville, New York: Reader's Digest Association, 1982.

Wetmore, Alexander. *Song and Garden Birds of North America.* Washington, D.C.: National Geographic Society, 1964.

INDEX